JESUS,
IN HIS OWN
WORDS

JESUS,
IN HIS OWN
WORDS

ROBERT H.
MOUNCE

B&H
PUBLISHING GROUP

NASHVILLE, TENNESSEE

978-1-4336-6919-4

Published by B&H Publishing Group
Nashville, Tennessee

Dewey Decimal Classification: 232.901
Subject Heading: JESUS CHRIST—BIOGRAPHY \
BIBLE. N.T. GOSPELS

1 2 3 4 5 6 7 8 • 14 13 12 11 10

To the two women in my life:
Jean, my loving wife for almost sixty years,
and our daughter Teri, radiant with joy

ACKNOWLEDGMENTS

I am indebted to so many throughout life whose words of encouragement and guidance have in a very real way had a part in this project. It could never have been written apart from the insights and influence of parents, family, friends, colleagues, and teachers. I am very much aware, as John Donne has it, that "No man is an island entire of itself."

More specifically I would like to acknowledge the recommendation of my friend Ray Clendenon (to whom I had submitted the manuscript) that the work be considered first by the trade division of B&H Publishing Group. It proved to be exactly the right thing. I also want to thank Tom Walters for his positive response to the project and to Kim Stanford for her careful and detailed editorial work.

CONTENTS

Chapter Seven: The Sermon on the Mount   51

Chapter Twenty-Nine: The Resurrection and Appearances 261

INTRODUCTION

You are about to read an account of the life and ministry of Jesus that combines all four Gospels into a single narrative and allows Jesus himself to tell us the story. Although the style is contemporary, the desire is to clarify the meaning of the original text rather than to impress the reader with clever phrases.

Having said that, the translation desires to provide a readable and accurate account, which will communicate the first-century message in contemporary language. Clarity has been a constant goal, and this involves making decisions regarding difficult verses and ambiguous language. The work falls clearly in the tradition of evangelical scholarship. Major guides have been Leon Morris on Matthew, Bill Lane on Mark, Darrell Bock on Luke, and D. A. Carson on John, and, of course, my own commentaries on Matthew (Hendrickson) and John (Zondervan).

Everyone who has studied the Synoptics realizes the multiple problems of repetition, overlap, and sequence. When the fourth Gospel is added, it becomes even more difficult. Did Jesus cleanse the temple early in his ministry as John says, or was it at the end of his ministry as the Synoptics have it? Or perhaps the temple was cleansed twice! Was the anointing of Jesus done in the house of Simon the leper (Matt. 26:6; Mark 14:3), in the home of a Pharisee (Luke 7:36), or in the home of Mary and Martha (John 12:1)? Who poured the ointment? Was it a woman of the city (Luke 7:37) or

Mary (John 12:3)? Did she pour it on his head (Matt. 26:7; Mark 14:3) or on his feet (Luke 7:38; John 12:3)? Or perhaps the varying accounts describe two (or three) different occasions.

All of this is to say that scholars hold different opinions regarding a number of items that surface when the four Gospels are compared. I have used my best judgment as guided by the insights of conservative scholars. In the vast majority of cases, it makes little difference as to where or when a particular teaching of Jesus occurs. For example, Matthew's Sermon on the Mount contains a dozen units, which are found scattered throughout Luke (primarily) in other historical settings. Jesus undoubtedly repeated himself on multiple occasions. Minor differences could be due to the specific occasion to which each writer refers or to how they remembered the words Jesus used.

In the case of the Sermon on the Mount, I have maintained Matthew's account as it is and allowed Luke the freedom of placing some of the units in other locations.

Good translation in the contemporary mode attempts to provide today's reader with an account that not only communicates accurately what Jesus did and said in the first century but also puts it in an idiom that has the same dynamic effect. The reader needs to "be there," whether on the hillside listening to Jesus talk about the kingdom or in a temple court castigating the scribes and Pharisees. I have taken the privilege of substituting for what might be called "standard" verbs others that seem to me to catch the dynamism of the moment. For example, the older brother of the prodigal son, when his father goes out and begs him to come in, "bursts out, 'All these years I have slaved for you . . .'" The standard "answered" for *apokritheis* simply will not do. I want demons to "shriek" and mobs to "shout." Whatever brings the story to life without calling undue attention to itself is used.

Some may say, "But aren't you interpreting," and the answer is yes. All translation involves interpretation. My prayer is that at no point have I misled in any way what Jesus was doing or saying. You will be the judge of that. Over forty years of translation, including major involvement in the NIV, NIrV, NLT, and the ESV (as well as consulting on the TNIV) have provided the foundation for this work.

It's obvious that sound theology must ultimately be built on the preferred texts in the original languages. I have wanted, however, for this translation to be usable as a preparatory step in that direction. So it comes with an extended table of contents and subject index. Should someone want to locate, let's say, the parable of the prodigal son, the table of contents will provide quick access to Luke 15:11–32. Should someone want to know what Jesus taught about divorce or about prayer, the index will take them to those specific verses. Here and there throughout the translation, I have added a phrase or sentence that provides historical or cultural context. All such additions are placed in brackets. One final item: cited at the close of each periscope are the Gospel references for that unit.

I trust that as you read this translation you will be aware that God continues to speak through his Word to all who have "ears to hear" (some biblical terminology defies change).

Robert H. Mounce

Chapter One

THE SETTING

―――――――∞――――――――

PROLOGUE

Before anything else existed, the Word already was—I am that Word. I was in fellowship with God; in fact, I was God. I was there from the very beginning. Through me God brought everything into existence. Not a single thing was created except that which was created through me. I am the source of all life, and that life has provided light for the human race. The light keeps on shining in the darkness, and the darkness has never been able to put it out.

At a crucial point in time, there came a man whose name was John the Baptist. He was sent by God to tell people about the light so they would come to believe through him. He himself was not that light but the one who was to tell others about the light.

The real light, which was destined to enlighten everyone, was about to come into the world. When I did enter the world, it failed to recognize me even though I had created it. I came to my own creation, but the very people I had created would not receive me. However, to as many as did receive me—that is, to those who believe that I really am who I claim to be—I gave the privilege of becoming sons of God. This new birth is not by natural means, the result of a physical impulse or because a man made a decision; it is a birth that comes from God.

I became a human being and lived like others. The disciples beheld my glory, the glory of the one and only Son, sent from the Father.

John the Baptist told everyone about me. He exclaimed, "He is the one I was talking about when I said, 'A man will follow me who is greater than I, for he existed even before I was born.'"

From my infinite supply of grace and goodness, those who believe have received one gracious gift after another. While the Law was given through Moses, it is through me, Jesus Christ, that grace and truth have come. No one has ever seen God. I myself am God and dwell in the presence of the Father. I am the one who told the disciples about God. *(John 1:1–18)*

JOHN THE BAPTIST TO BE BORN

During the reign of Herod, king of Judea, there was a priest named Zechariah ("God remembers") who belonged to the priestly division named after Abijah. His wife Elizabeth had also been born into the priestly line. Both of them were righteous in the sight of God, carrying out all the commandments and ordinances of the Lord blamelessly. But they had no children because Elizabeth was barren, and both of them were well along in years.

One day when his division was on duty and he was serving God in the temple, Zechariah was chosen by lot, as was the priestly custom, to enter the sanctuary of the Lord and burn incense. At the hour of incense, a large crowd of people had gathered outside and were praying.

While Zechariah was in the sanctuary, an angel of the Lord

appeared to him, standing on the right side of the altar. When Zechariah saw the angel, he was gripped with fear, visibly shaken. But the angel said, "Fear no longer, Zechariah, for God has heard your prayer; and your wife, Elizabeth, will bear a son for you. Give him the name John. He will bring you great joy and delight, and many will rejoice because of his birth, for he will be great as God counts greatness. He is never to drink wine or any other fermented drink, and he will be filled with the Holy Spirit even from his mother's womb. He will cause many in the nation of Israel to return to the Lord their God. Prior to the coming of the Lord, he will break onto the scene with the spirit and authority of the prophet Elijah. He will turn the hearts of the fathers back to their children and the disobedient to the good sense of the upright to prepare for the Lord a nation ready for his coming."

"But how can I be absolutely sure about this?" asked Zechariah. "After all, I am an elderly man, and my wife is getting along in years."

The angel replied, "I am Gabriel, and I have direct access to God. He is the one who sent me to tell you this good news. But now, because you did not accept without question what I said—and my words will come true at the appointed time—you will be unable to speak until the child is born." The people who were waiting for Zechariah to come out began to wonder why he stayed so long in the temple. When he did come out, he was unable to speak to them. They realized that while in the temple he had seen a vision because he kept making signs to them but could not utter a word.

When his period for priestly service was over, Zechariah left for home. Later on, his wife Elizabeth conceived and did not go out in public for five months. She said, "The Lord has looked with favor on me and taken away the disgrace I suffered in public by allowing me to have this child." *(Luke 1:5–25)*

MARY TO HAVE CHILD BY THE SPIRIT

Five months later God sent the angel Gabriel to Nazareth, a village in Galilee, to a young virgin by the name of Mary. (This is the Mary who would become my mother.) She was pledged in marriage to a man named Joseph, who was a descendant of King David. When Gabriel arrived, he said to Mary, "Greetings! The Lord is with you and has greatly blessed you!"

Mary was perplexed by what the angel said and wondered what the greeting could mean. Gabriel responded to her confusion, saying, "Don't be afraid, Mary, for God has been gracious to you. You will become pregnant and give birth to a Son, and you are to name him Jesus. He will be great and will be called Son of the Most High. The Lord God will make him a king as was his forefather David, and he will reign over Israel forever. His kingdom will have no end."

"How could I become pregnant," said Mary, "since I won't be living with Joseph as his wife prior to the marriage ceremony?"

The angel replied, "The Holy Spirit will come upon you, and the power of the Most High will cast his shadow over you. So the child to be born will be holy and will be called the Son of God. Did you know that your relative Elizabeth will also be giving birth to a child even though she is advanced in years? They said she couldn't have children, but she is already in her sixth month. God is fully able to carry out every promise he has ever made."

"Yes, I am the servant of the Lord," responded Mary. "Let this happen to me as you have said." Then the angel left. *(Luke 1:26–38)*

MARY VISITS ELIZABETH

A few days later Mary got ready and hurried off to a Judean town in the high country to the house of Zechariah. Upon arriving, she greeted Elizabeth, his wife. When Elizabeth heard Mary's greeting, the child in her womb leaped for joy, and Elizabeth was filled with the Holy Spirit. In great excitement she explained, "Blessed are you among women, and blessed is the child in your womb! Why am I so honored that the mother of my Lord should pay me a visit? Just think, the moment your greeting reached my ears, the babe in my womb leaped for joy. And blessed are you for believing that the Lord's promise to you will come to pass."

And Mary responded,

> My soul exalts the Lord,
> and my spirit rejoices in God my Savior;
> for he has looked with concern on his lowly servant.
> From now on all generations will call me blessed,
> for the Mighty One has done wondrous things for me.
> Holy is his name.
> From generation to generation he shows compassion
> to those who reverence him.
> He will do wondrous things with his powerful arm;
> He will scatter the arrogant with all their plans;
> He will bring down rulers from their thrones
> but exalt those of low estate;
> He will satisfy the hungry with good things,
> but send the rich away with nothing.
> He has come to the help of his servant Israel,
> remembering to be merciful to Abraham and his
> offspring forever, just as he promised our forefathers.

Mary stayed with Elizabeth about three months and then returned to her own home in Nazareth. *(Luke 1:39–56)*

JOHN THE BAPTIST IS BORN

The time for Elizabeth to have her baby arrived, and she gave birth to a son. When her neighbors and relatives heard that the Lord had shown such faithful love to her in removing her barrenness, they broke out in rejoicing with her.

Eight days later, as was the Jewish custom, they came to attend the circumcision ceremony. They were expecting his parents to name the boy after his father Zechariah, but his mother spoke up, "No," she said, "His name is to be John."

"But there is no one among your relatives that goes by that name," they objected.

So, by making various hand signals, they asked the baby's father what he would name him. Zechariah motioned for a wax tablet and, to the surprise of everyone, wrote, "John is his name." At that very moment Zechariah's mouth was opened, his tongue was set free, and he began to speak, praising God. All the neighbors were filled with awe, and the entire affair was discussed everywhere in the hill country of Judea. Everyone who heard about it took it to heart wondering, "What then will this child turn out to be?" For it is clear that the hand of the Lord is on him. Then his father, Zechariah, filled with the Holy Spirit, spoke this prophecy:

> Blessed be the Lord God of Israel,
> for he has come to his people and set them free.
> He has raised up a mighty Savior from the house of
> his servant David, just as he promised long ago
> through his holy prophets.
> His purpose was to save us from our enemies,
> and from all who hate us.
> He has shown us the mercy he promised to our
> ancestors.

He has kept his sacred covenant—the covenant he
swore with an oath to Abraham our father.
We have been delivered from our enemies.
Therefore, free from fear, we can serve him all the days
of our life in a holy and upright manner.
And you, my little child, will be called the prophet of
the Most High.
You will go ahead of the Lord to prepare the way for
him.
You will tell his people about salvation, about how they
can have their sins forgiven.
Because God is both merciful and tender, the bright
dawn of salvation is about to break upon us,
giving light to those who live in the dark shadow
of death, and guiding our feet into the way of
peace.

And the child continued to grow and became strong in body
and spirit. He lived in the desert until the day he made his public
appearance in Israel. *(Luke 1:57–80)*

MY FAMILY LINE ACCORDING TO MATTHEW

My family line begins with the patriarch Abraham and runs
through King David. Here it is:

The son of Abraham was Isaac. Then came Jacob, followed by
Judah and his brothers. Judah and his wife Tamar had Perez and
Zerah, the latter being the father of Hezron whose son was Ram.

Ram's son was Amminadab, who became the father of Nashon
and grandfather of Salmon. The son of Salmon and Rahad his wife
was Boaz, whose wife Ruth had a boy named Obed. Obed was the
father of Jesse, and Jesse was the father of David who became king.

After David came Solomon, by the wife of Uriah, then Rehoboam, Abijah, Asaph, Jehoshaphat, Joram, Uzziah, Jotham, Ahaz, Hezekiah, Manasseh, Amos, Josiah, Jechoniah, and his brothers. At this point in time, the Israelites were sent into exile in Babylon.

After the exile Jechoniah had a son named Shealtiel who was the father of Zerubbabel. From there on we have Abiud, then Eliakim, Azor, Zadok, Achim, Eliud, Eleazar, Matthan, and finally, Jacob, the father of Joseph, husband of Mary. Mary gave birth to Jesus who is called the Christ.

So there are fourteen generations between Abraham and David, fourteen from David to the deportation to Babylon, and fourteen from there to my birth. *(Matt. 1:1–17)*

Chapter Two

MY BIRTH AND BOYHOOD

MY BIRTH

My mother, Mary, was pledged in marriage to Joseph; but during the required year of waiting prior to the actual marriage, while she was still a virgin, it became apparent that she was pregnant. Joseph was a good man and reluctant to humiliate Mary in public [Deut. 22:23–27 calls for the stoning of a betrothed woman who's had sex with a man], so he planned to cancel the engagement quietly without pressing charges.

While he was considering this course of action, an angel of the Lord appeared to him in a dream and said, "Joseph, of the line of David, don't be afraid to take Mary home as your wife, for the child in her womb is by the Holy Spirit. She will give birth to a son, and you are to name him Jesus, for he will save his people from their sins."

This took place to fulfill what the Lord had promised through the prophet Isaiah: "Behold, the virgin will become pregnant and give birth to a son, and they will give him the name Emmanuel, which means 'God is with us.'"

13

When Joseph woke from sleep, he did what he had been told by the angel and took Mary home to be his wife. However, he allowed her to remain a virgin until she had given birth to a son whom he would name Jesus.

About that time an edict was sent out from Caesar Augustus [the first Roman emperor] that a census should be taken of the entire Roman world for the purpose of taxation. When this first census was taken, Quirinius was the governor of Syria. Everyone was required to return to their ancestral home in order to be registered.

Because he was a descendant of king David, my father, Joseph, went up from Nazareth in Galilee to Bethlehem in Judea [king David's town] to be registered. Mary, who was promised in marriage to him and was pregnant, went with him. While they were there in Bethlehem, the time came for Mary to have her baby. I was the child she bore, her firstborn. She wrapped me with strips of cloth and laid me in a feed box, for there was no room for us in the living quarters. *(Matt. 1:18–25; Luke 2:1–7)*

ADORATION BY SHEPHERDS AND WISE MEN

Not far away some shepherds were living out in the open fields, caring for their flock at night. Suddenly an angel of the Lord stood before them, and the glory of the Lord shone around them. They were terrified. But the angel said, "Don't be afraid! I bring you the good news of a great joy which is for everyone everywhere. This very night in the city of David, a Savior has been born for you; he is the Messiah, the Lord. This is how you will recognize him: you will find the infant wrapped with strips of cloth and lying in a feed bin."

Suddenly the angel was joined by a vast heavenly entourage singing praises to God and declaring, "Glory to God in the heavenly realms, and on earth peace among those he has favored."

When the angelic host left and returned to heaven, the shepherds said to one another, "Let's go straight to Bethlehem and see this wondrous event that the Lord has told us about!"

So they hurried to Bethlehem and searched until they found Mary and Joseph; and there I was, lying in the feed bin. When they saw me for themselves, they told others all that the angel had said to them about me. And everyone who heard it marveled at what the shepherds had told them. But Mary stored all these matters in her heart, often pondering how she could put them all together. Meanwhile, the shepherds returned to the fields, giving glory and praise to God for all they had heard and seen, just as the angel had told them.

At that time some wise men from the East arrived unexpectedly in Jerusalem, asking, "Where is the newborn king of the Jews? We saw his star when it first appeared in the East and have come to pay homage to him."

When reports of this reached king Herod, he was deeply disturbed, as was all Jerusalem. So he called together the chief priests and experts in the law and asked them if they knew where this king, the Messiah, was to be born.

"In Bethlehem of Judea," they answered, "for that is what God promised through Micah the prophet:

"And you, O Bethlehem, are not just a lowly village in Judah, because from you will come a ruler who will care for my people Israel."

Herod arranged a private meeting with the wise men and learned from them exactly when the star had appeared. Then he sent them back to Bethlehem saying, "Do your best to find the child, and when you have found him, let me know so I can come and worship him."

Having heard what the king had to say, the wise men went on their way. Suddenly the same star they had seen in the East appeared once again and led them until it came to rest directly above the place where I lay. When they saw the star, they were ecstatic with joy. They entered the house, and when they saw me in the arms of my mother, they fell to their knees and worshipped me. Opening their treasure chests they honored me with gifts—gold, frankincense, and myrrh.

Then they went back to their own country but by a different route because God had warned them in a dream against going back to Herod again. *(Matt. 2:1–12; Luke 2:8–20)*

CIRCUMCISION AND PRESENTATION IN THE TEMPLE

Eight days later, when I was circumcised, I was given the name Jesus, the name that the angel had assigned prior to my conception.

When the day for my mother's purification arrived, she and her husband Joseph took me to Jerusalem in order to present me to the Lord (Mosaic law requires that every firstborn male must be set apart to the Lord), and to sacrifice a pair of turtledoves or two young pigeons, as required by the law of the Lord.

At that time an elderly man by the name of Simeon was living in Jerusalem. He was an upright and devout man who was waiting eagerly the coming of the Messiah and the restoration of Israel that would follow. The Holy Spirit had disclosed to him that he would not die before seeing the Lord's Messiah. On that particular day the Spirit prompted Simeon to go into the temple courts. When Mary and Joseph arrived to dedicate me as their firstborn, a custom required by law, Simeon took me into his arms, praising God and saying: "Master, you may now let your servant die in peace, for I have seen with my own eyes the one who brings salvation. You have prepared him with all the nations in view: he is a light that will bring salvation to the Gentiles, and glory to your people Israel."

Upon hearing what Simeon said about me, Joseph and Mary were filled with wonder. He gave them his blessing and said to my mother, "Hear me now, many in Israel will either fall or rise because of your son. He will be a sign from God that many will reject and in so doing will reveal their secret thoughts. And sorrow, like a sharp sword, will pierce your heart as well."

There was also a prophetess in the temple courts by the name of Anna, the daughter of Phanuel, of the tribe of Asher. She was well advanced in years, having lived as a widow ever since her husband died after their marriage of seven years. Now she was eighty-four. She spent all her time in the temple, worshipping, fasting, and praying night and day. While Simeon was talking with my mother, Anna came by praising God. She told about me to all who were waiting for the redemption of Israel.

When my parents finished doing everything prescribed in the law, they returned to their hometown of Nazareth in Galilee. As time passed, I grew to maturity. I became strong and filled with wisdom, and the favor of God rested upon me. *(Luke 2:21–40)*

To Egypt and Back

When the wise men had left, an angel of the Lord appeared to Joseph in a dream. "Get up!" he said. "Take the child and his mother and go to Egypt. Herod is about to conduct a search for the child. When he finds him, he will put him to death. Stay there in Egypt until I let you know it's safe to return."

So Joseph got up, took Mary and me while it was still night, and left for Egypt. There we remained until the death of Herod. This fulfilled what the Lord said through the prophet Hosea: "Out of Egypt I have called my son."

When Herod realized that he had been tricked by the wise men, he became furious. He sent a detachment of soldiers to Bethlehem and the surrounding area with orders to kill all the male children two years and under. The timing was based on information he had gotten from the wise men regarding the first appearance of the star. This fulfilled what the prophet Jeremiah said: "In Ramah was heard the sound of weeping and loud wailing—Rachel grieving over the loss of her children. She refused to be comforted because they were no more."

After Herod died, an angel of the Lord appeared to Joseph in a dream and said, "Get up, take the child and his mother, and go back to the land of Israel; for those who wanted to kill your child have all died."

So my father got up, took my mother and me, and left for the land of Israel. *(Matt. 2:13–21)*

MY CHILDHOOD AT NAZARETH

However, when Joseph learned that Archelaus had become king over Judea in place of his father Herod, he was afraid to go there. Being warned in a dream, he went instead to the province of Galilee and settled in the town of Nazareth. So what the prophets said came true, "He will be called a Nazarene." There in Nazareth I grew up healthy and strong. I was full of wisdom and enjoyed the special attention of God. *(Matt. 2:22–23; Luke 2:39–40)*

TEACHING IN THE TEMPLE AS A BOY

Each year my parents went up to Jerusalem to celebrate the Passover so when I was twelve years old, we went up as usual. When the feast days were over, they started home to Nazareth, not notic-ing that I had remained in Jerusalem. Assuming that I was some-where in the caravan, they continued without missing me. When evening came, they began to ask relatives and friends if they'd seen me. Unable to find me, they returned to Jerusalem, looking for me all along the way.

Three days later they found me in the temple, sitting with the rabbis, listening to them and asking questions. All who heard me were astonished at my understanding and the skill with which I answered their questions. When my parents saw me engaged in conversation with the rabbis, they were dumbfounded. Mary burst out, saying, "Son, why have you treated us like this? Your father and I have been terribly worried about you. We've been searching everywhere."

I answered, "Why did you have to search for me? Didn't you know that I would be here in my Father's house?" But they failed to grasp what I was saying. Then I returned to Nazareth with my parents and continued to live under their authority. Mary took note of all that was happening and stored the memories in her heart. And I grew in both wisdom and stature, gaining the approval of God and all who knew me. *(Luke 2:41–52)*

Chapter Three

JOHN THE BAPTIST

JOHN THE BAPTIST

In AD 14, Tiberius Caesar became the second of the Roman emperors. Fifteen years later, the word of God came to John, son of Zechariah, while he was out in the Judean wasteland. At that time Pontius Pilate was governor of Judea, Herod Antipas [the son of Herod the Great] was tetrarch of Galilee, his brother Philip was tetrarch of the region northeast of the Sea of Galilee, and Lysanias was tetrarch of Abilene to the north. In the Jewish world Caiaphas was serving as high priest, but his father-in-law, Annas, who had preceded him, still exercised considerable influence.

John the Baptist traveled throughout the Jordan Valley proclaiming a baptism based on repentance, which led to the forgiveness of sins. He challenged all who came out to hear him to turn from their sins because the kingdom of heaven was about to appear.

The religious authorities in Jerusalem sent some priests and Levites to John to find out who he was. In answer to their question, John admitted with all candor, "I am not the Messiah."

"Then who are you?" they asked. "Are you Elijah?"

"I am not," he answered.

"Are you, by any chance, the prophet we have been waiting for?"

"No," he replied.

"Well then, who are you? Tell us so we can take the answer back to those who sent us. What do you say about yourself?"

John responded by quoting Isaiah the prophet:

> I am the voice of one calling out in the wilderness:
> Prepare the way for the coming of the Lord;
> > make his paths straight;
> > fill up the ravines and cut through the mountains;
> > straighten out the crooked roads and make the
> > > rough places smooth.
> The entire human race is about to see the glory of God.
> I am a messenger sent in advance to call the nation to
> > repentance.

For clothing John wore a rough coat made of camel's hair, tied at the waist with a rope of dried skin. For food he ate dried locusts and wild honey, food available in the wilderness. At that time people were coming out to him not only from Jerusalem but from everywhere in Judea and the entire Jordan Valley. As, one by one, they openly confessed their sins, he baptized them in the Jordan River. *(Matt. 3:1–6; Mark 1:1–6; Luke 3:1–6; John 1:19–23)*

JOHN PREACHES REPENTANCE

But when John saw a number of Jewish legalists and religious power brokers (the Pharisees and Sadducees) coming to be baptized, he rebuked them saying:

You bunch of snakes! Who led you to think you could escape the coming wrath of God? Show by your life that your heart has been changed. It's not enough to claim, 'Abraham is my father,' for in fact, God could produce descendants for Abraham out of even these lifeless stones. Even now, the ax of judgment is ready to sever each tree from its roots. So any tree that fails to bear good fruit will be cut down and thrown into the fire. *(Matt. 3:7–10; Luke 3:7–9)*

JOHN ANSWERS QUESTIONS

The crowd kept asking, "So what should we do?"

John answered, "Whoever has an extra shirt should give it to someone who has none, and whoever has food should share it with those who are hungry."

Some tax collectors, who had come to be baptized, asked John, "Teacher, what should we do to show that we have renounced our sins?"

John answered, "Stop collecting more tax than the Roman government requires."

Then some Jewish soldiers [assigned to assist and protect the tax collectors] asked John, "And how about us? How should we conduct ourselves?"

John's answer was direct and to the point, "Take money from no one by force or false testimony. Be content with what the job pays." *(Luke 3:10–14)*

JOHN'S MESSIANIC PREACHING

The hopes of the people began to rise as they pondered the possibility that this rustic prophet might be the long-awaited messianic

King. John dispelled the rumor publicly by declaring, "I am simply the one who baptizes you with water to show that you have turned from your sinful ways."

Some Pharisees responded, "So if you aren't the Messiah, or Elijah, or the prophet we have been waiting for, why are you baptizing?"

"I baptize only with water," answered John. "And although you do not recognize him, the one who is to come after me is right here among you. He is greater than I. I am not worthy to carry his sandals or even to bend down and untie them. He is the one who will baptize you with the Holy Spirit and fire. Even now he stands ready with winnowing fork in hand to separate every last grain of wheat from the chaff. The wheat he will store in the barn where it will be safe, but the chaff he will burn with an unquenchable fire." With these and many other challenging words, John proclaimed the good news to the crowds that were following him.

All this took place in the town of Bethany, east of the Jordan River where John was baptizing. *(Matt. 3:11–12; Mark 1:7–8; Luke 3:15–18; John 1:24–28)*

JOHN IN PRISON

Herod Antipas, governor of Galilee, had divorced his wife in order to marry Herodias, the wife of his half brother Philip. John the Baptist rebuked Herod for this immoral act ["It is not lawful for you to have her"], as well as for a number of other evil things he had done. Herod then topped them all by imprisoning John in the fortress, Machaerus, on the east shore of the Dead Sea. *(Matt. 14:3–4; Mark 6:17–18; Luke 3:19–20)*

MY BAPTISM

At that time I went from the town of Nazareth in Galilee to the Jordan River to be baptized by John. But John tried to talk me out of it, saying, "I ought to be baptized by you; why then are you coming to me for baptism?"

I answered him, "We will go ahead with the baptism, for that is the appropriate way to fulfill our righteous obligation."

So John baptized me. As I came up out of the water, the heavens opened, and I saw the Spirit of God descending like a dove and coming to rest on me. Then suddenly God's voice from heaven declared, "You are my own dear Son, in whom I take great pleasure."

The next day John saw me as I was walking along. "Look!" he called out, "The Lamb of God, the one who will take away the sin of the world! He is the one of whom I said, 'A man will follow me who is greater than I because he existed before I was born.' I didn't know that he was the coming one; but I have been baptizing with water so that God might reveal him to the people of Israel."

"I saw the Spirit," said John, "coming down from heaven like a dove and settling on him. I would not have known him, but the one who sent me to baptize with water said, 'The one on whom you will see the Spirit descending is the very one who will baptize with the Holy Spirit.' I saw this myself and therefore declare that this man is the Son of God." *(Matt. 3:13-17; Mark 1:9-11; Luke 3:21-22; John 1:29-34)*

MY FAMILY LINE ACCORDING TO LUKE

I was about thirty years of age when I began my public ministry. People regarded me as the son of Joseph, who was the son of Heli. [Matthew records my genealogy forward from Abraham through my father Joseph; Luke traces it back through my mother Mary to Adam. Luke was a companion of the apostle Paul, and one of the four writers to produce a "gospel" of my life and teachings. In preparing his account for the Roman official Theophilus, he investigated with care the many stories that were being passed on by my early followers: see Luke 1:1–4.]

The family line runs as follows: Joseph, Heli, Matthat, Levi, Melki, Jannai, Joseph, Mattathias, Amos, Nahum, Esli, Naggai, Maath, Mattathias, Semein, Josech, Joda, Joanan, Rhesa, Zeubbabel, Shealtiel, Neri, Melki, Addi, Cosam, Elmadam, Er, Joshua, Eliezer, Jorim, Matthat, Levi, Simeon, Judah, Joseph, Jonam, Eliakim, Melea, Menna, Mattatha, Nathan, David, Jesse, Obed, Boaz, Salmon, Nahshon, Amminadab, Ram, Hezron, Perez, Judah, Jacob, Isaac, Abraham, Terah, Nahor, Serug, Reu, Peleg, Eber, Shelah, Cainan, Arphaxad, Shem, Noah, Lamech, Methuselah, Enoch, Jared, Mahalalel, Kenan, Enosh, Seth, and Adam, the son of God. *(Luke 3:23–38)*

TEMPTED BY SATAN

After I was baptized, I left the Jordan River in the fullness of the Holy Spirit. I was led by the Spirit out into the wasteland to be tempted by the devil. I was there with wild beasts for forty days, fasting both day and night. As the time drew to a close, I was absolutely famished. Just then the Tempter came to me suggesting how I could satisfy my hunger: "You claim to be the Son of God, so why not simply say the word and these stones will turn into bread?"

I replied, "Scripture says, 'Man needs more than bread to live; he must also have the words that come from the mouth of God.'"

Then the devil took me to Jerusalem, the holy city, and had me stand on the highest pinnacle of the temple. He tempted me, saying,

"If it is true that you are the Son of God, then throw yourself down from here. After all, your Scripture says: 'God will send his angels to protect you,' and again, 'With their hands they will hold you up so you won't strike your foot against a stone.'"

Once again I replied, "But Scripture also says, 'Do not put the Lord your God on trial.'"

As a last recourse the devil took me to the top of a high mountain and showed me, in a single dazzling display, all the kingdoms of the world and their grandeur. He said, "All of this power and the glory that goes with it has been put in my hands, and I can give it to anyone I please. Here's my offer: I'll give it all to you on one condition—that you bow down and worship me."

Without hesitation I rebuked him saying, "Get out of here, Satan, for the Scriptures say, 'You are to worship the Lord your God and serve no one but him.'"

At this the Devil left me until a more favorable time would arise. Suddenly angels appeared and began to care for my needs. *(Matt. 4:1–11; Mark 1:12–13; Luke 4:1–13)*

Chapter Four

BEGINNING OF PUBLIC MINISTRY

THE FIRST DISCIPLES

The next day John the Baptist was standing outdoors with two of his disciples, and I walked by. "Look!" he exclaimed. "There is the Lamb of God!" When John's disciples heard him say that, they left him and came to me.

I turned and saw that they were following me, so I asked, "What do you want?"

"Rabbi," they said (the word means "Teacher"), "where are you staying?"

I answered, "Come along and you will see." So they came with me and saw where I was staying. Since it was about four in the afternoon, they stayed with me for the rest of the day.

Andrew, the brother of Simon Peter, was the other one who had heard what John said and had gone with me. The first thing he did was to find his brother Simon. "We have found the Messiah!" he told him (the word means "Christ," that is, "the anointed one").

29

Andrew brought Simon to me. Looking at him intently, I said, "You are Simon, the son of John; you are to be called Cephas" (the word means "Rock").

The following day I decided to go to Galilee. I said to Philip, "Come along with me." Philip was from Bethsaida, the town where Andrew and Peter lived.

Philip found Nathanael and told him, "We have found the one that Moses wrote about in the law, the one the prophets talked about. He is Jesus, the son of Joseph, and comes from the town of Nazareth."

"Nazareth!" exclaimed Nathanael. "Can anything good come from that place?"

Philip answered, "Come and see for yourself."

When I saw Nathanael approaching, I said, "Here comes a true Israelite, a man in whom there is no deceit!"

"How do you know me?" asked Nathaniel.

I answered, "I saw you when you were still sitting under the fig tree, before Philip spoke to you."

"Rabbi," exclaimed Nathaniel. "You are the Son of God! You are the King of Israel!"

"Is it because I told you that I saw you sitting under the fig tree that you believe?" I asked. "You will see greater things than that." Then I said to him, "The truth is that you will see heaven standing wide open and the angels of God coming down on the Son of man and going up from him." *(John 1:35–51)*

THE MARRIAGE AT CANA

Two days later Mary, my mother, went to a wedding in the Galilean town of Cana. Since I had been invited, I went to the wedding, and my disciples went with me. When the party ran out of wine, my mother came to me saying, "They don't have any more wine."

"I don't share your concern," I said. "My time has not yet come."

So my mother said to the servants, "Do whatever he tells you."

Nearby were six stone water jars, each capable of holding twenty to thirty gallons. The water was used for the Jewish custom of ceremonial cleansing. I told the servants, "Fill those six jars with water." So they filled them to the brim. "Now," I said, "dip some out and take it to the master of the feast."

The master of the feast didn't know where this wine that had been water had come from (but of course the servants knew), so he called the bridegroom aside and said, "People normally serve the best wine first, and then when the guests have had a bit too much to drink, they bring out a less expensive vintage. But you have saved the best until last."

This miracle, which I performed in Cana of Galilee, was the first of my miraculous signs. It revealed my divine nature and deepened the faith of my disciples. *(John 2:1-11)*

FROM CAPERNAUM TO JERUSALEM

After the wedding, I went to the town of Capernaum for a few days to be with my mother and brothers. My disciples were there as well. Since it was almost time for the Jewish feast of Passover, I left and went up to Jerusalem. *(John 2:12-13)*

MINISTRY IN JERUSALEM

When I was in Jerusalem during the festival of Passover, many people saw the miraculous signs I was performing and became convinced that I was, in fact, the promised Messiah. But I didn't trust myself to them because I knew what people were like. I didn't need any one to tell me about human nature because I fully understood what was in a person's heart. *(John 2:23–25)*

NICODEMUS LEARNS ABOUT THE NEW BIRTH

A man by the name of Nicodemus was a leader among the Jewish people. He belonged to the religious sect of the Pharisees. One night he came to see me and said, "Rabbi, we know that you are a teacher who has come from God, for no one could perform the miraculous signs that you are doing unless God were with him."

I replied, "I tell you the truth, unless a person is born again, he cannot see the kingdom of God."

Nicodemus asked, "How is it possible for a person to be born when he is old? Obviously, you can't enter your mother's womb and be born all over again."

I answered, "I tell you the truth, a person cannot enter the kingdom of God unless he is born of water and the Spirit. Physical birth results in a physical being; spiritual birth, in a spiritual being. You should not be surprised when I say that you must all be born again. The Spirit is like the wind, which blows wherever it wants. You can hear the sound it makes, but there is no way of knowing where it comes from or where it is going. Spiritual birth is like that."

"How could all this be?" replied Nicodemus.

I answered, "How is it that you, a highly respected Jewish teacher, don't understand these things? I tell you the truth; we know that what we talk about is true because we saw it ourselves. Yet you people will not accept what we say. If I speak of things on the earth and you don't believe me, how will you believe me when I talk of things in heaven?

"No one has ever gone up into heaven except the Son of man, the one who came from there. As Moses lifted up the bronze snake on a pole in the desert, so also must the Son of man be lifted up so that everyone who believes in him may have eternal life.

"This is how God loved the world: he gave his one and only Son so that everyone who believes in me will have eternal life and not die as a spiritual being. God did not send me into the world to pass judgment on it, but that it might be saved by me. Whoever believes in me is not condemned. However, the person who does not believe stands condemned already because he has refused to put his faith in me, God's one and only Son.

"Light came into the world, and rather than loving that light, people chose the cover of darkness because what they were doing was evil. People who do evil things hate the light. They won't come near it for fear that it will make clear to others what they are doing. On the other hand, those who live by the truth come willingly to the light. That way, everyone can see that what they are doing is done in fellowship with God."

After my conversation with Nicodemus, my disciples and I went out into the Judean countryside, where we stayed for a time baptizing believers. *(John 3:1–22)*

JOHN'S TESTIMONY TO ME

John the Baptist had not yet been put in prison but was at Aenon, near Salim. There was plenty of water there, and John was baptizing all the people who came to him.

Some of John's followers got into an argument with a Jewish man about the practice of ceremonial cleansing. So they came to John and asked, "Rabbi, the man you spoke about when you were east of the Jordan—the man you said was the Lamb of God—that man is now baptizing, and everyone is flocking to him."

John replied, "No one plays a role in the eternal plan unless it has been assigned to him by God. You yourselves heard me say, 'I am not the Messiah,' but rather, 'I have been sent as his forerunner.'

"In a wedding the bridegroom takes the bride. The role of the bridegroom's friend is to wait and listen for his coming. When he hears the voice of the bridegroom, he is overcome with joy. My joy is like that; it is absolutely complete. Jesus must become increasingly important, but I must fade away."

To this testimony by John, I added, "The one who comes from above is above all others. The one who belongs to the earth speaks only of things of the earth. I am the one from heaven. I speak of what I have actually seen and heard, yet none of you accept what I say. But whoever does accept my message has demonstrated his conviction that God is truthful. I was sent by God and speak the words of God, for God does not give his Spirit in limited measure.

"The Father loves the Son and has placed everything under his control. Everyone who puts his faith in the Son has eternal life. But no one who disobeys the Son will share in that life but will remain subject to the wrath of God." *(John 3:23–36)*

Chapter Five

EARLY MINISTRY IN GALILEE

BACK TO GALILEE

When I heard that John the Baptist had been put in prison, I left Judea and started back to Galilee, filled with the power of the Spirit. The Pharisees were aware that I was gaining and baptizing more converts than John, although it was my disciples, not I, who did the baptizing. *(Matt. 4:12; Mark 1:14a; Luke 4:14a; John 4:1–3)*

I TELL THE SAMARITAN WOMAN ABOUT LIVING WATER

My route to Galilee took me through Samaria. Before long I came to the town of Sychar located near the plot of land that Jacob had given to his son Joseph. Jacob had dug a well there. About midday, tired from my journey, I sat down beside the well to rest. A woman of Samaria came to draw water.

"Please give me some water to drink," I said. (My disciples had gone into town to buy food.)

The woman exclaimed, "How is it that you, a Jew, are asking me, a Samaritan, for a drink of water?" (No Jew would ever drink from a cup used by a Samaritan.)

I answered, "If you only knew the gift of God and who is asking you for water, you would be the one asking me, and I would give you living water."

The woman replied, "But sir, you don't have a bucket, and the well is deep. Where would you get this living water? Surely you can't be greater than our father Jacob? He is the one who gave us this well. He drank from it himself, and so did his sons and his flocks."

I replied, "Everyone who drinks of this water will get thirsty again, but once you drink of the water that I have to give, you will never be thirsty again. In fact, that water will become a perpetual spring bubbling up in you to eternal life."

"Please, sir," the woman exclaimed, "give me some of that water. Then I'll never get thirsty again, and I won't have to keep coming way out here to draw water."

I said, "Go and get your husband; then come back."

"I don't have a husband," she confessed.

"That's right," I said. "You don't have a husband. You've had five already, and the man you're living with now is not your husband. You told the truth."

Then the woman said, "Sir, I can see that you are a prophet! I have a question for you: Should we worship here on this mountain where our ancestors worshipped, or should we worship, as you, a Jew, would claim, in Jerusalem?"

"Believe me," I said to her, "the time is coming when the place where a person worships (here on this mountain or in Jerusalem) will no longer matter. You Samaritans know little about the one you worship, but we Jewish people know all about him because salvation comes through our race. A time is coming; in fact, it's already here, when true worshippers will be led by the Spirit to worship the Father as he really is. And the Father wants to be worshipped like that. God is spirit, and those who worship him must be led by the Spirit to worship him as he really is."

The woman said, "I know that the Messiah (who is called Christ) will come, and when he comes, he will explain everything to us."

"I am the Messiah," I said, "the very one who is speaking to you."

Just then the disciples returned from the town. They were surprised to find me talking with a woman. However, none of them asked her what she wanted or questioned me as to why I was talking with her. At that point the woman put down her water jar and hurried off to town, where she told everyone, "Come and meet the man who told me everything I have ever done! Could he really be the Messiah?" The people left what they were doing and hurried out to meet me.

Meanwhile, the disciples kept urging me to take some food and eat.

"I have a source of nourishment you know nothing about," I answered. They said to one another, "Could someone have brought him food to eat?"

I replied, "My food is to do what God wants. He is the one who sent me, and I must finish the work he gave me to do. You say, 'There are four months between sowing and harvest'; but I say, 'Open your eyes and look around! The fields are already ripe for harvest.'

"Already the reaper is drawing his pay for having gathered a crop destined for eternal life. Sowers and reapers are rejoicing together. The saying holds true, 'One sows and another reaps.' I am sending you to harvest a crop in a field where others have done all the hard work. You are about to reap the benefits of what they have done."

A number of people in Sychar came to believe in me because of the woman's testimony, "He told me everything I have ever done!" They came to me asking that I remain with them for a time. So for the next two days I stayed there, and many others believed when they heard me for themselves. To the woman they said, "We no longer believe just because you told us about him. Now that we have heard him for ourselves, we are convinced that he is the Savior of the world." *(John 4:4–42)*

MINISTRY IN GALILEE

Two days later I left Samaria and headed toward Galilee because, as I have often said, "A prophet is highly respected everywhere except in his own country" (in my case, Judea). When I arrived in Galilee, I was welcomed by the people because they had been at the festival in Jerusalem and seen everything I had done.

Some time later I moved from Nazareth where I had grown up, to the city of Capernaum on the shore of the Sea of Galilee, in the territory of Zebulun and Naphtali. This fulfilled what Isaiah prophesied of that region: "Land of Zebulun and land of Naphtali, on the road toward the sea, west of the Jordan, that part of Galilee where so many Gentiles live; you who are living in darkness will see a great light; on you who live in the dark land of death, the light will dawn."

From that time on I began to proclaim the gospel of God, saying, "The long-awaited hour has come; God is establishing his reign here on earth so turn from your sins and believe the good news." *(Matt. 4:13–17; Mark 1:14b–15; Luke 4:14b–15; John 4:43–46a)*

PREACHING AT NAZARETH

As I went from town to town in Galilee, I came to the village of Nazareth where I had spent my childhood. My disciples were traveling with me. On the Sabbath day I went to the synagogue as usual. The local authorities asked me to read from Scripture, so out of respect for the sacred text, I stood to my feet. I was handed the Isaiah scroll. I unrolled it and found the place that talks about God's anointed servant. I read, "The Spirit of the Lord is upon me because he has appointed me to preach good news to the poor. He has sent me to tell the captives, 'You are free!' and the blind, 'You will see again!' He has sent me to set free the victims of oppression and to proclaim that the time of God's salvation has come."

When I finished reading the passage, I rolled up the scroll, handed it back to the assistant and sat down to explain what it meant. The eyes of everyone in the synagogue were riveted on me. I said, "Today this passage of Scripture was fulfilled as you heard it being read."

Everyone was deeply impressed, both by my gentle demeanor and by the words I spoke, but were offended by what they implied—that I, a simple Galilean peasant, untrained in the rabbinic schools, was in fact the fulfillment of God's messianic promises through the prophet Isaiah. They marveled, "Where did this man get all this wisdom and the power to perform miracles? Isn't he the son of Joseph the carpenter? And isn't Mary his mother? Aren't James, Joseph, Simon, and Judas, his brothers, and don't his sisters live right here in Nazareth?"

I said to them, "You will probably quote me the saying, 'Doctor, heal yourself,' and challenge me to perform here in your town what you heard I did in Capernaum.

"But I tell you the truth, 'No prophet is highly respected in his own hometown, or among his relatives or even by his own family.'" I was astounded at their unbelief. It prevented me from doing miracles there, except I did lay hands on a few sick people and heal them.

"I tell you the truth," I continued, "In Elijah's day, when it didn't rain for three and a half years and the land suffered a great famine, there were many Jewish widows in Israel, yet Elijah was not sent to any of them. He went only to a Gentile widow living in the coastal village of Zarephath near Sidon. What's more, in the time of Elisha the prophet, there were many in Israel with leprosy, but none of them were healed; only Naaman, a general in the Syrian army."

When I reminded the people in the synagogue of God's care for the Gentiles, they became livid with rage. They broke up the meeting and dragged me out of town to the top of a nearby cliff intending to hurl me down. But at that point I walked straight through the crowd and left Nazareth never to return. *(Matt. 13:53–58; Mark 6:1–6a; Luke 4:16–30)*

THE CALL OF THE DISCIPLES

One day, as I was walking along by the Sea of Galilee, I saw two brothers, Simon (later on I named him "Peter") and his brother Andrew. They were getting ready to cast their nets into the water, for they were fishermen. "Come," I said, "be my disciples. I'll teach you how to fish for men." Immediately they dropped their nets and came with me.

A bit further on, I ran into another set of brothers, James, the son of Zebedee, and his brother John. They were sitting in a fishing boat with their father Zebedee, mending nets. When I challenged them to join me, they stopped what they were doing, left their father in the boat with his hired hands, and came with me. *(Matt. 4:18–22; Mark 1:16–20)*

TEACHING IN THE SYNAGOGUE IN CAPERNAUM

As we traveled on, we came to the city of Capernaum. When the Sabbath came, I went to the synagogue and began to teach. The congregation was taken aback at my teaching and considerably alarmed because I taught with authority, not like the religious scholars of the day. *(Mark 1:21–22; Luke 4:31–32)*

I HEAL A DEMONIAC IN THE SYNAGOGUE

As I was teaching, a man possessed by a demonic spirit suddenly shrieked out, "Leave us alone, Jesus, you Nazarene! You have nothing to do with us as yet. Have you come to destroy us? I know who you are—the Holy One of God."

I rebuked the evil spirit, saying, "Silence! I order you to come out of that man." The demonic spirit threw the man into convulsions right there before us. Then, with a deafening shriek, it came out without injuring him further.

The people were astonished. They began to ask one another, "What is this? Some new kind of teaching? With authority this man commands evil spirits, and they do what he says."

So this report about me spread quickly throughout all Galilee. *(Mark 1:23–28; Luke 4:33–37)*

PETER'S MOTHER-IN-LAW IS HEALED

Leaving the synagogue, I went straight to the house of Simon and his brother Andrew. James and John went with me. When we arrived, we learned that Peter's mother-in-law was ill with a high fever. So I went where she was lying and rebuked the fever. Her temperature dropped to normal, and the fever left. Then I took her by the hand and helped her to her feet. The first thing she did was to prepare a meal for us. *(Matt. 8:14–15; Mark 1:29–31; Luke 4:38–39)*

Evening in Capernaum

That evening after sunset (the Sabbath had just ended), people from all over Capernaum came to where I was staying. Crowding through the door, they brought me those who were suffering with various kinds of diseases as well as those who were possessed by demons. I laid my hands on each sick person, and every one of them was healed. This fulfilled what the prophet Isaiah said, "He took our weaknesses and carried away our diseases."

The demons who were cast out at my command shrieked, "You are the Son of God!"

I rebuked them and would not allow them to speak because they knew that I was the promised Messiah. *(Matt. 8:16–17; Mark 1:32–34; Luke 4:40–41)*

Preaching throughout Galilee

Early in the morning while it was still dark, I got up, left the house, and went to a lonely place where I could pray. Sometime later, Simon and his friends, realizing that I was no longer in the house, set out in search of me.

When they found me, they said, "Don't you know that everyone is looking for you?" Crowds of people had joined in the search, and when they located me, they tried to keep me from leaving the area.

I explained to them, "I must preach the good news about the kingdom of God in other towns as well. That is why God sent me. The time has come for me to leave you."

So I continued my journey throughout Galilee, teaching in synagogues and proclaiming the good news about the kingdom. People sick with every kind of disease were brought to me, and I healed them. *(Matt. 4:23; Mark 1:35–39; Luke 4:42–44)*

THE MIRACULOUS CATCH OF FISH

One day as I was teaching beside the Lake of Gennesaret (another name for the Sea of Galilee), people kept crowding in closer to hear what God had revealed to me. I noticed two boats moored at water's edge, left there by fishermen who were busy washing their nets. So I got into one of them, the one belonging to Simon, and asked him to push off just a bit from shore. Then I sat down in the boat and continued teaching the crowds.

When I had finished speaking, I said to Simon, "Now go out into deeper water where you and your crew can let down your nets for a catch."

"Master," Simon responded, "We worked hard all night long and caught nothing! But since you say so, we'll push out." Then when he ordered the nets let down, the crew pulled in so many fish that their nets began to break. They signaled men in the other boats for help, and together they loaded both boats to the sinking point.

When Simon Peter saw what had happened, he fell to his knees and cried out, "Leave me, Lord, for I am too sinful a man to be near you." Peter and the others with him were amazed at the remarkable size of the catch they had taken. So also were James and John, the sons of Zebedee who were partners with Simon in the business.

I said to Simon, "Don't be afraid; from now on you will be fishing for people." So they brought their boats to shore, left everything they had, and followed me. *(Luke 5:1–11)*

Chapter Six

FURTHER MINISTRY IN GALILEE

CLEANSING THE LEPER

When I came down from the hill country, I was met by a large crowd of people who followed me into a nearby city. A man there had a terrible skin disease that covered him from head to foot. Coming to me, he fell on his knees with his forehead to the ground. He pleaded, "Lord, if you are willing, you can make me clean."

Moved with pity, I stretched out my hand and touched him, saying, "It most certainly is my will! Be clean!" Immediately the ugly scars of leprosy vanished, leaving the man ceremonially clean once again. I told him not to tell others about this but to go immediately and show himself to the priest who would certify that he was cured. Then, as a witness to all that he was no longer afflicted with leprosy, he should offer the sacrifice required by Mosaic law.

But contrary to my instructions, he went out and began to tell everyone what had happened. The news that a leper had been healed spread rapidly. Soon I couldn't enter any town without attracting a crowd of people who hoped to hear me teach and be cured of whatever disease they had. Although I was staying out in the country, people who needed to be healed kept coming out to me from all the surrounding areas. Because of the crowds, I frequently withdrew to some deserted place to pray. *(Matt. 8:1–4; Mark 1:40–45; Luke 5:12–16)*

A Paralytic Is Healed

After this I went back across the lake to Capernaum, which I now considered my hometown. Within several days everyone knew that I was there, and crowds began to gather. Soon there was not enough room inside the house or even outside around the door to accommodate everyone. I preached the word to them, and the power of God was with me to heal.

One day four men arrived carrying a paralyzed man on a stretcher. They tried to bring him inside so they could lay him before me but were unable because the room was jam-packed. So they climbed up on the roof and removed the tiles directly above me. Then they lowered the paralytic through the opening.

I was profoundly impressed by the faith of the four men and what it led them to do. So I looked down at the paralytic lying on the stretcher and said, "Be of good cheer, my son! Your sins are forgiven."

At this the legal experts and the Pharisees were visibly upset. Cynically they asked, "Who is this man who dares to slander God like that? You heard him blaspheme! Certainly he knows that God alone, and no one else, can forgive sins."

When I saw how strongly they reacted, I asked why they were filled with such evil thoughts. "Tell me," I said, "which would be simpler—to say to this paralyzed man, 'Your sins are forgiven,' or 'Rise, take up your stretcher and walk?' So you will never have to question again whether the Son of man has the authority to forgive sins, I say to this poor man, 'Get up now, pick up your stretcher and go home.'"

Without hesitation the paralyzed man sprang to his feet, picked up his stretcher, and walked off praising God. The crowd was stunned. As the truth of what had happened began to sink in, a sense of awe swept over the crowded room. Everyone there began to glorify God for the power he had given me. They said, "Never have we seen such strange things as we have seen today." *(Matt. 9:1–8; Mark 2:1–12; Luke 5:17–26)*

THE CALL OF LEVI

After that, I went out along the sea where a crowd gathered to hear me teach. As I walked along, I caught sight of a Jewish tax official by the name of Levi. He was at work in his collection booth. "Come, be my disciple," I said. So Levi abandoned everything—business and all—got up, and came with me.

A bit later this same Levi prepared a feast, and I was the honored guest. He invited a large group of his friends—tax collectors and irreligious Jews—to share the feast with me. When the Pharisees and the legal experts who belonged to that party learned that I was eating with such people, they became righteously indignant. "Why does your teacher eat and drink with tax collectors and sinners?" they grumbled to my disciples.

I overheard the remark and replied, "People in good health don't need a doctor, but the sick do. Try to understand what God meant when, through the prophet Hosea, he said, 'It is mercy that I desire, not the sacrifice of some animal. I didn't come to call virtuous people to repentance, but sinners.'" *(Matt. 9:9–13; Mark 2:13–17; Luke 5:27–32)*

THE QUESTION ABOUT FASTING

One day when the disciples of John the Baptist were keeping a fast, some people came to me, somewhat perplexed, and asked, "Why is it that the disciples of John, as well as the disciples of the Pharisees, fast and pray on a regular basis, but your disciples don't fast at all? They just keep on eating and drinking as usual."

I answered this with a question: "Tell me, at a wedding would you expect attendants of the groom to fast while the groom was still there with them? Of course not! As long as the groom was still there, fasting would be ridiculous."

Then I showed how my way differed from tradition. "No one cuts a piece out of a brand-new coat and uses it to patch an old coat. If he did, the new coat would be left with a hole in it. Besides that, the patch would not match the old coat and would shrink and tear an even larger hole.

Here's another illustration: People don't pour wine that is still fermenting into old and brittle wineskins because the new wine would burst the old wineskins and spill out. What a loss! The new wine would be wasted and the old skins destroyed. No, new wine is kept in fresh wineskins; that way, both wine and wineskins will be preserved. But it appears that some have been drinking the old wine of tradition so long that they have no desire even to taste the new." *(Matt. 9:14–17; Mark 2:18–22; Luke 5:33–39)*

THE MAN WITH THE WITHERED HAND

One Sabbath I went to the synagogue as usual and began to teach. A man was there whose right hand was shriveled up. The Pharisees and legal experts watched me carefully to see if I would heal the man's hand on the Sabbath. If I did, they would have a basis for leveling a charge against me. I knew all along what they were scheming, so I said to the man with the withered hand, "Come here and stand where everyone can see you."

Then I turned to those who were anxiously watching and posed this question: "If your only donkey, ox, or sheep should fall into a pit, would you not get it out without delay, even though it was the Sabbath? Of course you would! Surely this man is of greater value than a donkey or a sheep!

"I ask you, is it lawful on the Sabbath to do good [as I intend to do] or to do harm [as your view of the Sabbath would lead you to do]—to restore this man's hand or leave it withered as it is?" Dead silence filled the room.

I was deeply distressed by their indifference to human distress. Looking around the room at each of them in anger, I said to the man, "Stretch out your withered hand" (an act beyond what the crippled man could do). The man stretched out his right hand, and at once it was fully restored, as sound as the other.

The Pharisees stormed out of the synagogue, filled with rage. Immediately they began to lay plans with the Herodians [those sympathetic to the crafty Herod Antipas], as to how they could get rid of me for good. *(Matt. 12:9–14; Mark 3:1–6; Luke 6:6–11)*

Choosing the Twelve

A few days after that I went up onto the mountain to spend the night in prayer. When morning came, I called my disciples together and chose twelve of them, whom I named apostles. I wanted them to be my closest companions, to learn from me and then go out and proclaim my message. I gave them authority to cast out demons. They are: Simon (I named him Peter), and Andrew his brother, James and his brother John (sons of Zebedee, I called them Boanerges or "Men of Thunder"), Philip, Bartholomew, Matthew and Thomas, James the son of Alphaeus, Simon, who was called the Zealot, Judas the son of James (Thaddeus), and Judas, who would betray me. *(Mark 3:13–19a; Luke 6:12–16)*

Chapter Seven

THE SERMON ON THE MOUNT

THE SETTING

My reputation spread quickly beyond the boundaries of Galilee, and soon people were coming to me from every part of the surrounding area. People suffering from every known kind of illness and severe pain were brought to me, and I healed them. They struggled to touch me because the healing power that came from me was working such miracles. Demoniacs, epileptics, and paralytics were all cured of their disabilities. Consequently, huge crowds followed wherever I went—people from Galilee, the district of the Ten Towns (Decapolis), Jerusalem, all Judea, the seacoast of Tyre and Sidon, as well as the land east of the Jordan River.

When I saw the crowds, I went up the mountainside and sat down, as rabbis do when they teach. My disciples gathered around me, and I taught them as follows: *(Matt. 4:24–5:2)*

THE BEATITUDES

"How blessed are those who recognize their spiritual need, for the kingdom of heaven belongs to them alone.

"How blessed are those who understand the sorrow of this world, for God himself will comfort and encourage them.

"How blessed are those who don't promote themselves, for to them life yields its rewards.

"How blessed are those who long to do what pleases God, for God will satisfy them completely.

"How blessed are the compassionate, for God will be compassionate to them.

"How blessed are those whose hearts are pure, for they alone will see God.

"How blessed are those who work for peace, for God will call them 'my sons.'

"How blessed are those who are persecuted for doing what God desires, for the kingdom of heaven belongs to them.

"How blessed you are when others revile you and persecute you and spread all kinds of vicious slander about you because you have taken up my cause in a sinful world. Rejoice and shout for joy because great is your reward in heaven; for that is how they persecuted the ancient prophets." *(Matt. 5:3–12)*

SALT OF THE EARTH

"You are the salt of the earth, but if salt loses its saltiness, there remains no way to make it salty again. Since it is no longer good for anything, it is thrown out and trampled underfoot." *(Matt. 5:13)*

LIGHT OF THE WORLD

"You are the light of the world. A city built on a hill cannot be hidden. People don't light a lamp and then hide it under a basket.

They put in on a lamp stand so every one in the house can see. Let your light shine like that for others so they may see the good you do and praise your Father who is in heaven." *(Matt. 5:14–16)*

THE LAW AND THE PROPHETS

"Don't think for a moment that I have come to do away with the sacred law of Moses or the writings of the prophets. My role is to show the kind of life they were intended to produce. I came to fulfill them, not to abolish them. I tell you for a fact that until heaven and earth pass away not even the smallest letter—or even a part of that letter—will be removed from the law until it has been completely fulfilled. So whoever disregards one of these commandments, even the least important, and teaches others to do the same will be regarded as least in the kingdom of heaven; but whoever keeps them and teaches others to follow his example will be highly regarded in the kingdom of heaven. For I tell you that unless your righteousness goes beyond the legalism of the scribes and Pharisees, you will never enter the kingdom of heaven." *(Matt. 5:17–20)*

MURDER AND WRATH

"You have heard that it was said to people in former days, 'Do not commit murder,' and 'Whoever murders will be taken to court.' But I say: 'Anyone who harbors anger against his brother will answer for it in court; whoever maligns his brother (e.g., "You numskull"), will have to appear before the highest court, and whoever says, "You cursed fool!" is headed straight for the fire of hell.'

"So if you are involved in an act of worship and suddenly remember that your Christian friend has some grievance against you, leave your gift there at the altar, and before you do anything else, go to him and try to be reconciled. Then come back and continue your act of worship.

"If someone has a claim against you, come to terms with him quickly while you still have a chance. Once you are in court, your opponent may turn you over to the judge and the judge to a guard who will put you in prison. There you will remain, count on it, until you have paid the last penny of your debt." *(Matt. 5:21–26)*

ADULTERY AND DIVORCE

"You have heard the commandment, 'Do not commit adultery.' But I say that anyone who looks at a woman with sex on his mind has already committed adultery with her in his heart. So if your right eye causes you to sin, gouge it out and throw it away because it is better for you to lose that one member of your body than to have the entire body thrown into hell. Or if your right hand leads you to use it for some sin, cut it off and throw it away because it is better for you to lose that one member than to have the entire body thrown into hell.

"It was also said, 'Whoever divorces his wife is required to give her a written notice of divorce.' But I say that if a man divorces his wife, except on the ground of sexual infidelity, he makes her a partner in adultery when she marries again, and the man who marries this 'divorced' woman is also guilty of adultery." *(Matt. 5:27–32)*

OATHS

"You have also heard that our ancestors were taught, 'Don't break an oath, but carry through on the promise you made when you invoked the name of the Lord.' But I tell you: Don't bind yourself with an oath at all; do not swear by heaven, for it is the throne of God, nor by the earth, for that is where God rests his feet, nor by the city of Jerusalem, for that is where the great king lives. Don't swear by your own head because you can't make even a single hair white or black. Simply answer 'Yes' or 'No' and mean it. Anything beyond that is the work of the evil one." *(Matt. 5:33–37)*

RETALIATION

"You have heard that it was said, 'Only an eye for an eye and only a tooth for a tooth.' But I say: Don't resist the one who wants to harm you. Instead, if he slaps you on the right cheek, turn the other to him as well. And if someone takes you to court to get your shirt, give him your coat as well. And if a soldier of an occupying force wants you to carry his gear for a mile, carry it for two. Give to the one who comes to you begging, and don't turn your back on the one who would borrow from you." *(Matt. 5:38–42)*

LOVE OF ONE'S ENEMIES

"You have heard that it was said, 'Love your neighbor'—and that's fine—'but it's OK to hate your enemy.' But I tell you something quite different: Love your enemies as well as your neighbors. Pray for those who persecute you. That way you will demonstrate to others that you are true sons of your Father in heaven. He makes his sun rise on sinners as well as on saints and sends rain to water the fields of both the honest and the dishonest. Now if you love only those who love you, what reward is there in that? Even the despised tax collectors manage that much. And if in the marketplace you greet only your friends, what are you doing more than anyone else? Even the Gentiles do that? Since your heavenly Father is even-handed in his relationship to all, you, his children, are to love your enemies as well as your friends." *(Matt. 5:43–48)*

ALMSGIVING

"Be careful not to make a show of your religion, for if you do, you will receive no reward from your Father in heaven. For example, whenever you give something to a needy person, don't call attention to it by blowing a trumpet. That's what the hypocrites do in their synagogues and on the street corners. They do it for the applause they get, and you can be sure that that is all the reward they will get. But when you perform a charitable act, keep it to yourself; not even your left hand should know what your right hand is doing. In that way your gift will be truly private, and your Father who knows full well what you do in private will reward you." *(Matt. 6:1–4)*

PRAYER

"When you pray, don't be like the hypocrites, for they love to stand up in the synagogues so others can see them pray. They choose the busiest street corners in town as places to pray so that others can't help but see how pious they are. You can be sure of this; they have already received the reward they're going to get.

"But when you pray, go into a room by yourself. When you have shut the door, pray to your Father who is with you there in the secret place, and your Father who sees what you are doing in secret will reward you." *(Matt. 6:5–6)*

THE LORD'S PRAYER

"One more thing, when you pray, don't babble on and on, repeating phrases grown tired with use. That's how some people pray because they think God will be impressed with their many words and listen to them. You don't need to pray long prayers because your Father already knows what you need, even before you ask him.

"Here is how you should pray:

> 'Our Father in heaven,
> may your name be held in honor,
> may your kingdom come and your will be
> done here on earth as it is in heaven.
> Give us each day the bread we need for that day,
> and forgive us our sins as we ourselves have forgiven
> those who have sinned against us.
> Keep us from those trials we can't handle,
> and deliver us from the evil one.'

"For if you forgive others their sins, your Father in heaven will also forgive you; but if you refuse to forgive others, then your Father will not forgive you your sins." *(Matt. 6:7–15)*

FASTING

"When you fast, don't go around looking gloomy like the hypocrites. They disfigure their faces so others will be sure to notice that they are fasting. Believe me, they already have all the reward they are going to get. Now as for you, when you fast, brush your hair and wash your face like you normally do; that way people will not even suspect that you are fasting. Of course, your Father will know because he watches what you do that is unnoticed by others, and he will reward you." *(Matt. 6:16–18)*

TREASURES

"Stop storing up treasure here on earth where everything is either wearing out or apt to be stolen. A far better way is to store up your treasure in heaven where nothing like that can happen. The important point is that wherever you store your treasure is where your heart is going to be." *(Matt. 6:19–21)*

THE SOUND EYE

"The eye is like a lamp for the body. It follows that if your eye is clear it will allow the entire body to be filled with light. On the other hand, if your eye is cloudy, your whole body will be dark. If the light you think you have is actually darkness, how deep is that darkness." *(Matt. 6:22–23)*

SERVING TWO MASTERS

"A slave cannot serve two masters at the same time; he will love the one (i.e., be loyal to him) and hate the other (i.e., have nothing to do with him). It is impossible to serve both God and financial gain." *(Matt. 6:24)*

ANXIETY

"Therefore I tell you not to worry about such little things as whether you will have enough to eat and drink or whether you will have something to wear. Certainly there is more to life than food and clothing. Consider the wild birds: they don't plant seeds, harvest a crop, or store it all in a granary. Your heavenly Father takes care of that. Think about it; aren't you of greater concern to God than the birds? Can any of you by worrying add even one hour to your life?

"And why do you worry about clothing? Look at the wild flowers in the fields, how they grow. They're not hard at work making their own clothing, yet I can assure you that not even Solomon dressed in his royal robes could match the beauty of one of these. Now if God clothes the fields with such beautiful flowers, which are alive today but gone tomorrow, burned in the oven, is he not much more likely to clothe you? How slow you are to trust him! So stop worrying about things such as where your food will come from, or if you'll have enough to drink, or what you will wear for clothing. Nonbelievers make things like that the primary goal of life, but in your case your heavenly Father already knows you need them, and he will take care of it.

"But more important than anything else is that you set your heart on his kingdom and what he desires of you. If you do, he will provide you with all the other things. So don't worry about tomorrow; each day will have enough worries of its own." *(Matt. 6:25–34)*

JUDGING

"Don't be sharply critical of others, or God will judge you in the same way. You know, don't you that you will be judged by the same standard that you use in judging others? The same rules will apply to you that you apply to others.

"Why do you draw attention to the tiny bit of sawdust in your brother's eye when you've got a huge log protruding from your own? Perhaps you think it possible to remove sawdust from someone else's eye while blinded by a log in your own? You phoney! Get rid of the log in your own eye and only then will you see clearly enough to remove the sawdust from your brother's eye." *(Matt. 7:1–5)*

PROFANING THE HOLY

"Do not give what is holy to unholy people, or, like dogs, they will turn and attack you. Do not put what is precious before pigs, or they will trample it under their feet." *(Matt. 7:6)*

GOD ANSWERS PRAYER

"Ask, and God will give it to you; search, and you will find; knock, and the door will be opened for you. For the one who keeps on asking receives, and the one who searches diligently finds, and the one who won't stop knocking that will have the door opened to him.

"No father among you, if his son should ask for some bread to eat, would give him a stone. Or if he should ask for a fish would hand him a snake. So if you, bad as you are, know how to give good things to your children, how much more will your heavenly Father give what is good to you!" *(Matt. 7:7–11)*

THE GOLDEN RULE

"The way you want others to treat you is exactly the way you should treat them. This way of living fulfills everything required by the law and prophets." *(Matt. 7:12)*

THE TWO WAYS

"The path to heaven leads through a narrow gate. That's the way you must go. If you follow the crowd down easy street through the broad gate, you're headed toward destruction. The gate to life is narrow, and the road is difficult; not many find it." *(Matt. 7:13–14)*

"BY THEIR FRUITS ..."

"Watch out for religious phonies; they come to your gatherings disguised as sheep, but underneath they are wild wolves intent on tearing you apart. You can recognize such people by watching how they live. Thornbushes do not yield grapes, and briars do not produce figs. In the same way, a healthy tree will bear good fruit, and a rotten tree will bear bad fruit. Healthy trees can't bear bad fruit, and rotten trees can't bear good fruit. It is that simple. So a religious teacher whose life fails to bear good fruit will be cut down and thrown like a dead branch into the fire of judgment. The way to find out whether a person is genuine is to look at how he lives." *(Matt. 7:15–20)*

"SAYING, LORD, LORD"

"Not every person who calls me, 'Lord, Lord,' will enter the kingdom of heaven, but only those who actually do what my heavenly Father requires. When the Day of Judgment comes, many will say to me, 'Lord, Lord, didn't we prophesy in your name, and wasn't it in your name that we cast out demons and performed many miracles?'

"Then I will tell them face-to-face, 'You were never friends of mine. Get out of my sight, you evil doers.'" *(Matt. 7:21–23)*

THE HOUSE BUILT UPON THE ROCK

"So everyone who listens to my words and acts on them is like a wise man who builds his house on solid rock. Before long the rain comes pouring down, the floodwaters rise, and the wind beats hard against the house, but it does not collapse because it is founded on rock. However, everyone who listens to my words and does not act on them is like a foolish man who builds his house on sand. Sooner or later the rain will come pouring down, the floodwaters will rise, and the wind will beat hard against the house. The house built on sand will collapse, and great will be its fall." *(Matt. 7:24–27)*

THE CROWD RESPONDS

When I finished my discourse, the crowd was astonished at what I had been teaching them. Unlike their own religious scholars, I spoke with authority. *(Matt. 7:28–29)*

Chapter Eight

THE SERMON ON THE PLAIN

SETTING

I came back down the mountain with the Twelve and stopped for a while in a broad open area. People from all over Judea, from Jerusalem, and from the coastal region of Tyre and Sidon gathered to hear me teach and to be healed of their diseases. Even those tormented by evil spirits were cured. Everyone in the crowd was trying to touch me because it was obvious that I possessed the power to heal.

Looking up at those who had gathered around, I said . . . *(Luke 6:17–20a)*

THE BEATITUDES

"How blessed are you who own nothing, for the kingdom of heaven belongs to you.

"How blessed are you who hunger now, for God will satisfy you completely.

"How blessed are you who weep now, for you are going to laugh.

"How blessed you are when men hate you, when they exclude you, when they insult you and curse you as evil because you are my followers.

"Rejoice when that happens; leap for joy because your reward in heaven is great. That is exactly how your fathers treated the prophets." *(Luke 6:20b–23)*

THE WOES

"How sad it is for you who are wealthy now because you have already received all the happiness due you.

"How sad for you who have eaten your full because you are going to get hungry.

"How sad for you who are laughing now because you will come to mourn and weep.

"How sad for you when everyone speaks well of you because that's exactly what their fathers did to the false prophets." *(Luke 6:24–26)*

LOVE OF ONE'S ENEMIES

"But to those of you who are not like that, I say, Love your enemies, do good to those who hate you, bless those who curse you, and pray for those who mistreat you. If someone slaps you on one cheek, offer him the other as well. If someone takes your coat, offer him your shirt as well. Give to everyone who asks, and when someone takes what belongs to you, don't try to get it back. Treat others as you would like them to treat you. What special merit is there in loving those who love you? Even sinners do that. And what credit do you get for doing good to those who are good to you? Even sinners do that. And why should you receive a blessing for lending to those who are sure to repay? Even sinners lend to one another when full repayment is certain.

"No, God calls on us to love our enemies. We are to do good to them, to lend and expect nothing in return. Then our reward will be great, and others will see what it means to be a son of God. For he is kind to the ungrateful and the wicked. Be compassionate, just as your Father is compassionate." *(Luke 6:27–36)*

JUDGING

"Stop judging others, and God will not judge you. Don't condemn others, and God won't condemn you. Forgive others, and God will forgive you. Give to others, and God will give to you. He will pour into your lap a generous measure, pressed down, shaken together, and overflowing. The measure you use for others is the measure that God will use for you.

"It is obvious that a blind man can't guide another blind man. Should he try, would not both of them wander off and fall into a pit? No disciple is better informed than his teacher; however, once his training is complete, he will be like his teacher.

"Why do you point out the speck of sawdust in your brother's eye but pay no attention to the huge log that is sticking out of your own eye? Can't you see how ridiculous you look when you offer to remove sawdust from your brother's eye but can't see past the log in your own? You hypocrite! Begin by removing the log from your own eye, and then you will see clearly enough to remove the bit of sawdust from your brother's eye." *(Luke 6:37–42)*

"BY THEIR FRUITS . . ."

"A healthy tree does not bear rotten fruit, nor does a diseased tree bear good fruit. Each tree is known by the fruit it produces. If you want figs, you don't go to a thornbush to pick them. Grapes are not gathered from a bramble bush.

"The good man lives a productive life, drawing on the good which is stored in his heart, but the evil man expresses by his evil acts the wickedness stored in his heart. What a person says reveals what he is treasuring in his heart.

"So why do you keep calling me 'Lord, Lord,' when in fact you don't live the kind of life I require?" *(Luke 6:43–45)*

THE HOUSE BUILT UPON THE ROCK

"There are two ways to build a house. One way is to dig down through the soil until you reach solid rock and lay the foundation there. This kind of builder not only listens to what I have to say but also puts my teaching into practice. When the storm comes and the floodwaters rise, the house stands firm. It can't be shaken, built as it is on a solid foundation. The other way to build is not to forget all about a foundation. This kind of builder listens to what I have to say but doesn't put it into practice. As you would expect, when the storm comes and the floodwaters rise, this house collapses and is swept downstream." *(Luke 6:46–49)*

Chapter Nine

HEALING MINISTRY IN GALILEE

THE CENTURION OF CAPERNAUM

When I finished the Sermon on the Plain, I went to Capernaum. In that city was a centurion of the army of Herod Antipas who had a servant whom he held in high regard. Unfortunately the servant was seriously ill, disabled by paralysis and confined to bed. Racked with pain, the servant was about to die. When the centurion learned that I had come back from Judea and was there in Galilee, he sent a group of prominent Jewish friends to ask me to come and heal his servant. When they arrived, they pleaded earnestly with me, saying, "The centurion deserves this favor because he is a good friend of our people. For example, he built a synagogue for us at his own expense."

"Unless you people see miracles and wonders," I said, "you will never believe!" But the emissaries begged me to come so I agreed.

But before I arrived at the centurion's house, I was met by another group who explained that it wasn't necessary for me to come all the way to the house. In the words of the centurion, "Lord, don't trouble yourself, for I am not worthy to have you under my roof. That is why I didn't come to you in person. Just give the order, and my servant will be healed. I understand the role of authority. I myself am under superior officers, and I have soldiers under me. I say to one, 'Go,' and he goes, and to another, 'Come here,' and he comes. When I tell my servant, 'Do this,' he does it. Just say the word and my servant will be restored."

I was amazed to hear these words from a secular army officer, a Gentile. Turning to the crowd, I said, "Never before have I encountered faith like this, not even among Jews. And I assure you that many non-Jews will be at the messianic banquet from all over the world. They will sit down to feast with Abraham and Isaac and Jacob in the kingdom of heaven; while Israelites, presumably the heirs of the kingdom, will be expelled into outer darkness where they will weep and grind their teeth."

Then I sent the delegation back to the centurion with this message: "It will been done for you, just as you believed it would." Arriving back at the house, the group learned that the servant had been healed at that very moment when I spoke the word, at one o'clock the previous afternoon. The centurion and everyone in his family became believers. *(Matt. 8:5–13; Luke 7:1–10; John 4:46–54)*

THE WIDOW'S SON AT NAIN

Soon after this my disciples and I went to the village of Nain. A great number of people followed us. As we neared the entrance to the town, we were met by a funeral procession. The one who had died was the only son of his mother, now a widow. When I saw her, my heart was moved with compassion. "Do not weep," I said. Reaching out, I placed my hand on the coffin as it was passing by, and the procession came to a stop. "Young man," I said, "wake up!" The corpse sat up and began to talk. Then I presented the formerly dead son to his mother. The crowd could scarcely believe their eyes. They raised their voices in praise to God exclaiming, "A great prophet has arisen in our midst! God has shown how he cares for his people." News of this remarkable event spread like wildfire throughout Judea and the surrounding countryside. *(Luke 7:11–17)*

STILLING THE STORM

That evening I got into a boat with my disciples and said, "Let's cross to the other side of the lake." So we set sail along with several other boats. After we had gone some distance, a fierce storm suddenly arose. Huge waves crashed over the deck. Even though the craft was about to break apart and sink, I was asleep on a cushion in the stern. The frightened disciples rushed back to me and woke me with their cries of, "Lord, save us! We're going to die! Don't you care if we perish?"

Calmly I said to them, "Why are you so easily frightened by a storm? You trust me so little!" Then I got up and ordered the wind and the waves to cease. Suddenly everything was perfectly calm.

The disciples shook their heads in amazement, asking themselves, "What sort of man is this? Even the wind and the waves obey his command!" *(Matt. 8:23–27; Mark 4:35–41; Luke 8:22–25)*

THE GADARENE DEMONIAC

As we were getting out of the boat on the other side of the lake, in the region of the Gerasene, we were met by a man with an unclean spirit. He no longer lived like others in a house but had gone into the burial caves near the city. He went about stark naked and was so violent that no one dared go near him. The townspeople had tried to restrain him with chains but were unable. He had often been shackled with fetters and bound with chains, but he broke the fetters into pieces and wrenched the chains apart. No one was strong enough to keep him under control. And so day and night he wandered among the tombs and on the hillsides howling and gashing himself with sharp stones.

When he saw me from a distance, he came running and flung himself at my feet. I knew the man was under the control of an unclean spirit, so I said. "Come out of that man, you evil spirit!"

Speaking through the man, the evil spirit screamed back, "What do you want with me, Jesus, Son of the Most High God? In God's name I implore you, do not torment me before the appointed time."

I asked, "What is your name?"

"Legion," he answered, "my name is Legion because there are so many of us." Then he begged me not to send him out of the country or into the abyss.

Nearby on a hillside was a large herd of pigs feeding. The evil spirits pled, "If you are going to cast us out, please send us to that herd of pigs."

So I said, "Go then."

The demons came out of the man and went into the pigs. Then the entire herd of some two thousands pigs rushed in panic down the steep bank and into the lake where they drowned.

When the herdsmen saw what had happened, they fled, telling the story everywhere. As a result the report spread quickly throughout the area. Many came to me, and when they saw the demoniac sitting there, clothed and in his right mind, they were filled with fear. Eyewitnesses told them what had happened to the demoniac and the pigs. Their reaction was to beg me to leave their neighborhood, so great was their fear.

As I was getting into the boat, the demoniac came and asked to go with me, but I refused him." I said, "Go back to your friends and tell them how much the Lord has done for you, how he has had mercy on you." So he left and began to tell everyone throughout the ten towns what I had done for him. Everyone was amazed. *(Matt. 8:28–34; Mark 5:1–20; Luke 8:26–39)*

JAIRUS'S DAUGHTER AND THE WOMAN WITH A HEMORRHAGE

I left the land of the Gerasene and sailed back across the lake. Coming ashore on the western side, I was received enthusiastically by the crowd that had been waiting for me to return. While I was still there by the lake, an official of the local synagogue by the name of Jairus came and knelt before me. "My little daughter is dying," he exclaimed urgently. "She is only twelve, my only child. I beg you to come to my house and lay hands on her so she will recover and live."

So I rose and left with my disciples for the home of Jairus. A large crowd followed us.

En route we were met by a woman who had suffered with a life-threatening flow of blood for more than a dozen years. Although she had suffered a great deal under the care of many doctors and spent all her resources, she had not gotten any better. In fact, she had grown worse. She had heard the reports about me and was sure that if she could only touch my cloak, her bleeding would stop, and she would be ritually clean once again.

As I was passing by, the woman slipped up from behind and touched one of the tassels of my cloak. Immediately her flow of blood stopped, and she could feel in her body that she had been healed. Aware that healing power had gone out from me, I turned to the crowd and asked, "Who touched me?"

Peter and the other disciples replied, "Master, you see all the people crowding in from every side! How could you ask who touched you?"

But I kept trying to locate the person. "Somebody touched me," I said, "because I felt healing power go out."

When the woman grasped what had happened to her and that she could not escape notice, she came and threw herself at my feet, frightened and shaking all over. There in front of everyone, she explained why she had touched me and how she had been healed at that very moment.

"Take heart, my daughter," I said, "your faith has made you well. Go in peace and be freed from your suffering."

While I was still speaking, some men came from the house of the synagogue official to tell him the sad news that his daughter had died. "Why bother the Master any further?" they added. At that point I turned to Jairus and said, "Don't lose your courage; just continue to believe, and she will be all right."

Then I turned the crowd away and allowed no one to go with me except Peter, James, and his brother John.

Before long we arrived at the home of Jairus where we found people weeping and wailing unrestrainedly. Professional mourners and hired musicians were busy carrying out their expected roles. Going into the house, I asked the crowd, "Why are you making such a commotion? The child is not dead; she is only sleeping."

They laughed at me because they were there when it happened and knew for sure that she had died.

So I took my three disciples and the girl's parents and went to where the girl was lying. Reaching out, I took the girl by the hand and raised her to her feet. To the child I said, *"Tabitha cumi,"* which means (in Aramaic), "Little girl, I say to you, arise!" Immediately the girl arose and began to walk about. She was thirteen at the time. Those who saw it were overcome with excitement. I gave them strict orders that no one should be told about what had happened. Then I instructed the parents to give her something to eat. The report, however, soon spread throughout the entire countryside. *(Matt. 9:18–26; Mark 5:21–43; Luke 8:40–56)*

Two Blind Men

Another day as I was walking along, two blind men came up behind me, crying out, "Take pity on us, Son of David! Take pity on us!" When I got to the place where I would be staying, the blind men went right inside with me. So I asked them, "Do you believe that I can cure your blindness and make you see once again?"

"Yes Lord, we do," they answered.

So I touched their eyes and said, "Because you believe it will happen, it will."

And suddenly they could see again! They were so excited that I cautioned them sternly not to let anyone know what had happened. But they kept singing my praises everywhere they went. *(Matt. 9:27–31)*

Chapter Ten

THE TWELVE DISCIPLES

THE DUMB DEMONIAC

As we were leaving the house, some people brought me a man unable to talk because he had a demon. Once I had cast out the demon, the man began to speak, and everyone who heard him was astonished. They exclaimed, "We have never seen anything like this before in Israel." *(Matt. 9:32–34)*

THE HARVEST IS GREAT

I continued on my way through the towns and villages of Galilee, teaching in their synagogues, proclaiming the glad news that God reigns supreme, and healing diseases of every kind. My heart was filled with compassion for the people who crowded around me, for they were confused and helpless, like sheep without a shepherd. I said to my disciples, "The harvest is great; many are ready for the kingdom; but there are only a few workers. So ask the Lord, to whom the harvest belongs, to send out workers into the fields and bring in the grain." *(Matt. 9:35–38)*

COMMISSIONING THE TWELVE

Then I selected twelve disciples and gave them the authority to cast out demons and cure diseases and illnesses of every kind. I chose:

Simon (also known as Peter)

Andrew (Peter's brother)

James, the son of Zebedee

John (the brother of James)

Philip

Bartholomew

Thomas

Matthew the tax collector

James the son of Alphaeus

Judas the son of James (Thaddaeus, Lebbaeus)

Simon the Zealot (or the Cananean)

Judas Iscariot (who later betrayed me)

These twelve I sent on a mission. I said, "Don't go to Gentile regions or even to the towns of Samaria, but go to the lost sheep of the house of Israel. Tell them that the kingdom of heaven is at hand. Heal those who are sick, bring the dead to life, cleanse the lepers, cast out demons.

"You have received freely, so give freely. Leave your money belt at home; you won't need any gold, silver, or even copper. Don't carry a traveling bag with a spare shirt or an extra pair of sandals. Don't even bother with a staff. The worker deserves his keep.

"When you come to a town or village, look for someone who is open to the message of the kingdom and stay with him until you leave that town. When you enter his house, pronounce the blessings of God on it. If the family is deserving, may the peace of God come upon it; but if not, may your greeting return to you. And if there is no one in that town who will welcome you or listen to the message of the kingdom, then, as you leave, shake the dust of the town off your feet. Believe me, on the Day of Judgment, God will show more mercy to Sodom and Gomorrah than to the people of that town.

"When you find yourself like sheep surrounded by a pack of wolves, remember that I am the one who sent you on the mission. So be as wise as snakes yet as innocent as doves." *(Matt. 10:1–16)*

THE FATE OF THE DISCIPLES

"Watch out for those who have the authority to hand you over to the local council because they can flog you up to thirty-nine lashes right there in the synagogue.

"Because you are my followers, you'll have to stand trial before the highest officials in the land, even before kings. On such occasions tell the Gentile world the message of the coming kingdom.

"Whenever you are brought to trial, don't worry about what kind of defense you should make or how to present it. When the time comes, God will tell you what to say. So, although you will be the one saying the words, it will actually be the Spirit of your Father, the Holy Spirit, who will be speaking through you.

"Hostility will become so extreme that family loyalties will disappear. A brother will betray his own brother to death. Even more tragic, a father will turn against his own child. Children will take the stand against their parents and sign their death warrants.

"Because of your allegiance to me, you will be hated everywhere you go. Remain faithful because it is the one who stands firm to the end that will be saved. However, you should not try to become a martyr; if they persecute you in one town, move on quickly to the next. Believe me when I tell you that you will not have fulfilled your mission throughout the towns of Israel before I, the Son of man, return victorious from the grave.

"It is everywhere understood that a student is not superior to his teacher or a slave to his master. The student must accept the fact that he cannot be treated better than his teacher, and the slave, that he'll be spared the opposition met by his master. If they called me Beelzebul, the 'Prince of Evil,' and I am the master of the house, how much more will they malign you, the members of my household!" *(Matt. 10:17–25)*

DON'T FEAR TO SPEAK OUT

"Do not be afraid of men who oppose you, for in the end you will be vindicated. Every evil act they have covered up will be brought to light; every one of their secret plans will be disclosed to all. What I tell you now in private, shout out loud in broad daylight; what I whisper in your ear, proclaim from the roof of your house.

To you my friends, I say, "Do not fear those who can do no more than kill the body and after that are powerless. I will tell you whom to fear: Fear God! He has the authority not only to kill you but after that to throw you into hell. Believe me, he is the one you ought to fear!

You can buy two little sparrows in the marketplace for a penny or two. Yet should one of them, cheap as they are, fall to the ground, your Father will know about it. So don't be afraid of those who oppose you; you are far more important to God than hundreds of sparrows. He is concerned about every single hair on your head—he counts them!

Anyone who confesses in public that he belongs to me will be acknowledged by me in the presence of God's angels. But anyone who denies in public that he belongs to me will be denied by me in the presence of God's angels. *(Matt. 10:26–33; Luke 12:2–9)*

A Gospel That Divides

"Don't think that I have come to bring peace to the world. I bring conflict, not peace. From now on the truth of the gospel will divide like a sharp sword, even between members of the same family. A family of five will be split three against two, son against father, and daughter against mother. My message will separate mothers-in-law from daughters-in-law. A person's worst enemies will turn out to be members of his own family." *(Matt. 10:34–36; Luke 12:51–53)*

Conditions of Discipleship

"Anyone who cares more for his father or mother than for me is not worthy of me. Anyone who cares more for his son or daughter than for me is not worthy of me. Whoever refuses to take up his cross and follow me wherever I go is not worthy of me." *(Matt. 10:37–39)*

Rewards of Discipleship

"Whoever welcomes you as you travel through Galilee welcomes me, and anyone who welcomes me welcomes the one who sent me. Whoever receives a prophet because he is a prophet will receive a prophet's reward, and whoever receives a just man because he is just will receive a just man's reward. The one who gives even a cup of cold water to someone of less importance because he is a disciple will never lose his reward."

After delivering these instructions to my twelve disciples, I went out and continued my ministry of teaching and preaching throughout Galilee. *(Matt. 10:40–11:1)*

JOHN'S QUESTION AND MY ANSWER

When the disciples of John the Baptist told him everything I was saying and doing, John sent two of them to me with the question, Are you the one I have been saying would come, or are we supposed to wait for someone else? At that time I was curing all sorts of diseases, healing many who were suffering from plagues and casting out evil spirits. Even the blind were having their sight restored.

When John's disciples arrived, they posed the question, and I answered, "Go back and tell John what you have seen and heard— that the blind are made to see, the lame start to walk, lepers are being cleansed, the deaf can hear, the dead are raised up, the poor have the good news proclaimed to them. How blessed is the one who takes no offense at me." *(Matt. 11:2–6; Luke 7:18–23)*

MY WORDS ABOUT JOHN

Once the messengers left, I began to talk to the crowd about John. "What did you go out into the desert to see? A blade of grass blown back and forth by every breath of wind? Tell me, what did you go out to see? Certainly not a man adorned in luxurious clothing. People like that live in palaces. So what did you go out to see? Was it not a prophet? Yes indeed. And the prophet you saw was far more than a prophet: he is the one of whom Scripture says, "Behold, I am sending my messenger ahead of you to open the way for you.

"Of all the children born to women, there has never been one greater than John; yet the most humble person in the kingdom of God is greater than he."

"Up until the time of John the Baptist, the law of Moses and the writings of the prophets were in effect. Since then the kingdom of God has been proclaimed, and all are urged to enter it. The law, however, hasn't been discarded. It would be easier for heaven and earth to pass away than for a single bit of the law to disappear."

Now everyone who heard me say this, including the tax collectors, agreed that God was right, for they had accepted John's baptism. But the Pharisees and the legal experts thwarted God's purpose by refusing to be baptized by John.

"How can I describe these people? They are like boys hanging out in the marketplace. They yell at another, 'Hey, we took our flutes and played wedding music, but you wouldn't dance. So we played funeral music, but you wouldn't mourn.' In the same way, when John the Baptist came fasting and abstaining from wine, you said, 'He has a demon.' But when the Son of man came and didn't fast or abstain from wine, what did you say? 'Look at that man! He is a glutton and a wine drinker, a friend of tax collectors and other outcasts.' Yet wisdom is shown to be true in the lives of those who accept it." *(Matt. 11:7–19; Luke 7:24–35)*

WOE TO THE CITIES OF GALILEE

I began to criticize openly the cities in which I had done most of my miracles because they didn't repent of their sins.

"Woe to you, Chorazin! Woe to you, Bethsaida! If the miracles done in you had been done in wicked Tyre or Sidon, they would have repented long ago in sackcloth and ashes. But mark my word; it will be more tolerable on the Day of Judgment for Tyre and Sidon than for you. And you, Capernaum, will you be exalted to heaven? No, your fate is to be thrown down to Hades, the place of the dead. If the miracles that were done among you had been done in Sodom, that town would still be standing. You can be sure of this, Capernaum, it will be more tolerable on the Day of Judgment for Sodom than for you." *(Matt. 11:20–24)*

Chapter Eleven

TEACHING IN GALILEE

THANKSGIVING TO THE FATHER

Inspired with joy by the Holy Spirit, I prayed: "I praise you, Father, Lord of heaven and earth, that although you have hidden these truths from the wise and discerning, you have made them known to the childlike. Yes indeed, Father, for that is how you wanted it to be.

"My Father has handed over everything to me. No one knows the Son except the Father just as no one knows the Father except the Son and anyone to whom the Son decides to reveal him." *(Matt. 11:25–27; Luke 10:13–15)*

"COME TO ME ..."

"Come to me, all you who are weary with the burdens of life, and I will give you the rest that refreshes. Take on a yoke like mine, and let me show you how to meet life. Then your soul will be renewed, for I am gentle and humble in spirit. The yoke I wear fits so well that the load you carry will seem light." *(Matt. 11:28–30)*

PLUCKING GRAIN ON THE SABBATH

One Sabbath during harvest season, my disciples and I were walking by a wheat field. They were hungry and began to pick grain and eat it. Nearby were some Pharisees who were watching to see what we might do. When they saw my disciples threshing the grain by rubbing it between their hands, they came to me and asked, "Why are your disciples doing what the law forbids on the day of rest?" [Rabbinical rules considered plucking wheat as reaping, rubbing it between the hands as threshing, and blowing away the chaff as winnowing—all work forbidden on the Sabbath.]

I asked them, "Haven't you read in the Scriptures what David and his men did when they needed something to eat, how they entered the tabernacle during the priesthood of Abiathar and ate the sacred bread set out before God? What they did was against the law because only the descendants of Aaron were allowed to eat the sacred bread.

"Or haven't you read in the law how the priests are in violation of the Sabbath rest when, each week, they perform sacrifices in the temple? But no one holds them guilty! I tell you, something far greater than the temple is here. Scripture clearly says that God desires mercy, not the sacrifice of animals. If you really understood this, you would not have been so quick to condemn innocent men of reaping on the Sabbath.

"The Sabbath was made for the sake of man, not man for the Sabbath. For this reason the Son of man is sovereign over the Sabbath." *(Matt. 12:1–8; Mark 2:23–28; Luke 6:1–5)*

I HEAL MULTITUDES BY THE SEA

Aware of their plot to kill me, I withdrew with my disciples to the shores of Lake Galilee. Huge crowds from Galilee and Judea, as well as the city of Jerusalem, followed us. Many others came from as far away as Idumea, the seacoast of Tyre and Sidon, and beyond the Jordan River. The crowds that came out to hear me teach and heal were so large that I had the disciples keep a small boat ready to escape being crushed. I healed every sick person who came to me and cured all who were tormented by unclean spirits. The crowd kept pressing forward, hoping to touch me because it was obvious that I had the power to heal. Whenever a person with an unclean spirit came, he would fall to the ground and cry out, "You are the Son of God." But I rebuked the demons and charged them not to speak or reveal who I was.

This fulfilled what God had said through his prophet Isaiah:

> Here is my servant whom I have chosen,
>> the one I love, in whom I delight;
> I will put my Spirit on him,
>> and he will proclaim a time of judgment for the
>>> nations.
> He will not quarrel or cry out;
>> nor will anyone hear his voice in the streets.
> A bruised reed he will not break,
>> nor a smoldering wick he will not snuff out,
>> till he leads justice to victory.
> In his name the nations will put their hope.
> *(Matt. 12:15–21; Mark 3:7–12; Luke 6:17–19)*

A LESSON IN DEVOTION

One day a Pharisee invited me to dine with him so I went to his house and sat down to eat. In that same town lived a woman who was a sinner. When she learned that I was having dinner at the Pharisee's house, she brought an alabaster flask of perfume and came to where I was sitting. She began to weep as she knelt behind me. Her tears flowed down onto my feet so she unloosened her hair and used it to dry them. She kissed my feet repeatedly and anointed them with the perfume.

When the host saw what was happening, he said to himself, "If this man were really a prophet, he'd know what sort of woman is touching him—that she is a sinner."

I knew what he was thinking so I said to him, "Simon, I've got something to say to you."

"What is it, Rabbi?" he answered.

"There was a money lender who had two debtors: one owed him five hundred silver coins and the other fifty. Neither was able to pay him back so he cancelled the debt of both. Which one, do you think, was the more appreciative?"

"I imagine it would be the one who was forgiven the most," he answered.

"Right you are," I said. Then pointing to the woman, I said, "Simon, do you see this woman? When I came into your house, you poured no water on my feet, but she has literally bathed my feet with her tears and dried them with her hair. You didn't welcome me with the customary kiss, but from the time I sat down she has not stopped kissing my feet. You neglected the courtesy of anointing my head with oil, but she has anointed my feet with expensive perfume. Therefore, I tell you that her sins, which were many, are forgiven, as shown by her love. But the one who is forgiven little shows only a little love." Then to the woman I said, "Your sins are forgiven." Those at dinner with me began to wonder out loud, "Who is this that even forgives sins?"

To the woman I said, "Your faith has saved you; go in peace." (Luke 7:36–50)

WOMEN WHO HELPED

After this I traveled through the nearby towns and villages proclaiming the good news of the reign of God. The twelve disciples were with me. So also were some women who had been set free from evil spirits and infirmities. Among them were Mary Magdalene, from whom seven demons had been expelled, Joanna the wife of Cuza (Herod's business manager), Susanna, and many other women who helped support us using their own resources. *(Luke 8:1–3)*

MY SANITY QUESTIONED

Then I returned to Capernaum, and crowds gathered so quickly that there wasn't even time to eat. When my family in Nazareth heard what was going on, they came to take me away by force. "He has lost control of his senses," they explained. *(Mark 3:19b–21)*

ON COLLUSION WITH SATAN

Just then a demon-possessed man, blind and unable to speak, was brought to me. I cured him, and he began both to speak and to see. The crowd was amazed and questioned whether I could be the promised Son of David.

But the religious leaders who had come down from Jerusalem said, "No. This man is possessed by Beelzebub, the prince of demons, and that's where he gets the power to cast out demons." Others, to test me, asked for a sign from heaven.

I was fully aware of what my antagonists were thinking, so I asked them to consider how unreasonable it would be for Satan to cast out Satan. They would agree that a kingdom at war with itself cannot stand. Or that a family or a village that keeps quarreling cannot stay together. In the same way, if Satan should rise up against himself, how could his kingdom survive?

"You said that it is from Beelzebub that I get the power to cast out demons. Suppose, for the moment, that you're right—the power to cast out demons comes from Beelzebub. Then where did your exorcists get their power? Your own disciples won't accept an argument like that. However, if it is by God's Spirit that I am casting out demons, then it is evident that the kingdom of God has in fact arrived.

"As long as a strong man [Satan] is fully armed, he can guard his own castle, and his possessions will be safe. But when someone even stronger [the Son of Man] attacks and defeats him, he will take away the weapons the strong man relied on and carry away his possessions. To steal a strong man's belongings, you must first render him helpless.

"Whoever is not with me is against me, and whoever does not help me gather is scattering." *(Matt. 12:22–30; Mark 3:22–27; Luke 11:14–23)*

THE SIN AGAINST THE HOLY SPIRIT

"Every form of sin and blasphemy will be forgiven with one exception—the sin of blasphemy against the Spirit. Whoever speaks against the Son of Man can be forgiven, but whoever speaks against the Holy Spirit can never be forgiven in this age or in the age to come." I said this to the religious leaders because they were claiming that I had an unclean spirit.

"To have good fruit you must grow a healthy tree. If your tree is not good, its fruit will not be good. The condition of the tree is shown by the kind of fruit it bears.

"You brood of snakes! How can you say anything good since you are evil? What you say reveals what you have treasured in your heart. The good man lives a productive life, drawing upon the good which is stored in his heart, but the evil man expresses by his evil acts the wickedness stored within. I tell you, on the Day of Judgment, each of you will have to answer for every thoughtless word you have ever spoken. You will be declared innocent or guilty on the basis of the words you have spoken." *(Matt. 12:31–37; Mark 3:28–30; Luke 11:17–23)*

THE SIGN OF JONAH

As the crowds kept growing, some of the legal experts and Pharisees came to me asking for a sign. I answered, "It is an evil and adulterous generation that asks for a sign. No sign will be given to you except the sign of Jonah. As Jonah was a sign for the men of Nineveh, so will the Son of Man be a sign for this generation. Just as Jonah spent three days and three nights in the belly of a sea monster, so will the Son of Man be in the heart of the earth for three days and three nights.

"When the Day of Judgment comes, and this generation is on trial, the Queen of the South will take the stand and leave you without excuse because she came all the way from a distant country to learn the wise teaching of King Solomon. Now one greater than Solomon is here, but you refuse to listen. When the Day of Judgment comes and you're on trial, the men of Nineveh will take the stand and leave you without excuse because, when Jonah preached, they repented. One greater than Jonah is now here, and you refuse to repent." *(Matt. 12:38–42; Luke 11:29–32)*

THE EVIL SPIRIT RETURNS

"Whenever an evil spirit leaves a person, it wanders about in arid places looking for someplace to rest. Finding none, it says, 'I will go back where I came from.' When it returns, it finds its former residence unoccupied, swept clean, and all in order. So it goes out, finds seven other spirits more evil than itself, and brings them back to live there. So that person is worse off than he was before. And that is exactly what will happen to this evil generation." *(Matt. 12:43–45; Luke 11:24–26)*

MY TRUE FAMILY

I was still speaking when suddenly my mother and brothers arrived. Unable to get through the crowd, they sent a message asking me to come out and speak with them. But I said, "Who is my mother, and who are my brothers?" Then glancing around and pointing to my disciples, I said, "Look, these are my mother and my brothers. Whoever does the will of God, my Father in heaven, is my brother, my sister, my mother." *(Matt. 12:46–50; Mark 3:31–35; Luke 8:19–21)*

Chapter Twelve

MY PARABLES

That same day I left the house where I was staying and went out along the lakeshore. I sat down to teach those who had come from the neighboring towns to listen. The crowd grew so large that I had to get into a small boat so I could be heard by all the people gathered on the shore. I taught them many spiritual truths using simple stories from everyday life. Here is one of them:

THE PARABLE OF THE SOWER

"One spring day a farmer went out into his field to plant a crop. As he scattered the seeds, some fell along the path where they were either trampled underfoot or snatched away by hungry birds. Other seeds landed on rocky ground where there was little soil. They sprouted quickly because the soil was shallow, but after a few days of hot sun, they were scorched. Having no strong roots, they withered and died. Other seeds fell among thistles that grew up and chocked the life out of them. Some seeds, however, fell on rich soil and produced a bumper crop; sometimes a hundred to one, sometimes sixty, and sometimes thirty. Anyone who wants to learn should pay attention." *(Matt. 13:1-11; Mark 4:1-9; Luke 8:4-8)*

WHY I USE PARABLES TO TEACH

One day when I was sitting by myself, some from the crowd who had heard me teach came with the Twelve to learn about parables and why I used them to teach.

I told them, "The privilege of understanding the secrets of the kingdom of heaven has been given to you, but not to others. To those who have, more will be given, and they will have more than enough; but from those who have nothing, even the little they have will be taken away. I use parables in speaking with the crowds because, although they have eyes, they don't really see, and although they have ears, they don't really hear or understand. If they did, they would turn to God and be forgiven. So in them the prophetic words of Isaiah are finding fulfillment:

No matter how often you hear, you will never
understand,
or look and you will never comprehend.
For your minds have become sluggish,
your ears are hard of hearing,
and your eyes have been closed.
If that weren't true,
you would see with your eyes,
hear with your ears,
and understand with your mind.
Then you would turn to me,
and I would heal you.
(Matt. 13:10-17; Mark 4:10-12; Luke 8:9-10)

UNDERSTANDING THE PARABLE OF THE SOWER

"If you don't understand the parable of the sower, you won't be able to understand any of the other parables. So listen while I explain it.

"The seed is my teaching about the kingdom. Some of it lands along the path; that is, it is heard but not understood. In this case the evil one comes and snatches away the seed that was sown in one's heart.

"The seed that fell on rocky ground represents the person who hears the word and accepts it with enthusiasm. But he lacks depth and cannot hold out for long. When persecution comes because of the message, he quickly turns against it.

"The seed sown among thistles stands for people who hear the message, but the worries about this life and the deceitful nature of wealth strangle it so it yields nothing.

"Finally, the seed sown in rich soil is the person who hears the message and understands it. He produces a bumper crop—sometimes a hundred to one, sometimes sixty, and sometimes thirty." *(Matt. 13:18–23; Mark 4:13–20; Luke 8:11–15)*

"HE WHO HAS EARS TO HEAR, LET HIM HEAR"

"No one lights a lamp and then covers it with a basket or puts it under the bed. Lamps are to be put on lamp stands so that those who enter the room may see. Nothing is hidden that will not in time be brought out into the open or covered that will not be made known and brought to light.

"Take heed what you hear; the measure you use for others will be the measure God uses for you, and he will give you even more. For to those who have, more will be given; but from those who have

nothing, even the little they think they have will be taken away."
(Mark 4:21–25; Luke 8:16–18)

THE PARABLE OF THE SEED GROWING SECRETLY

"Here is another parable to help you understand what the kingdom of God is like.

"It is like a man who scatters seed in a field. Then during the day while he is busy with his chores as well as at night while he is sleeping, the seeds sprout and begin to grow. The man doesn't understand how it all happens; but the soil, all on its own, produces the crop—first the tender shoot, then the head, and in time the head full of grain. When the grain is ripe, the man takes his sickle and begins to reap because harvest time has come." *(Mark 4:26–29)*

THE PARABLE OF THE WEEDS

"The kingdom of heaven is like a man who sowed good seed in his field, but one night while everyone was fast asleep, an enemy came and sowed weeds among the wheat, then slipped away. When the wheat sprouted and heads of grain began to form, the weeds appeared as well. The man's servants came to him and said, 'Master, was it not good seed that you sowed in your field? So where did these weeds come from?'

"He answered, 'Some enemy must have done it.'

"The servants asked, 'Do you want us to go out and pull up the weeds?'

"'No' he replied, 'because when you are pulling up weeds, you may uproot some wheat as well. Better to let them both grow together until the harvest. Then I will tell the workers to pull the weeds up first, then tie them in bundles to be burned. After that they can gather the wheat and put it into my barn.'" *(Matt. 13:24–30)*

THE PARABLE OF THE MUSTARD SEED

I asked, "So what is the kingdom of God like? To what can I compare it so that it will be simple enough for you to understand?

"The kingdom of heaven is like a mustard seed which was planted in a garden. It is the smallest of all the seeds, yet when planted and fully grown, it becomes the largest bush in the garden, a veritable tree with branches so large that the birds of the air come and make their nests in its shade." *(Matt. 13:31–32; Mark 4:30–32; Luke 13:18–19)*

THE PARABLE OF THE FERMENTED DOUGH

I asked again, "What else is there to which I can compare the kingdom of God? It is like fermented dough which a woman took and worked into a bushel of flour until the whole batch had risen." *(Matt. 13:33; Luke 13:20–21)*

WHY I SPEAK IN PARABLES

When talking to the crowds, I always speak in parables. I tell them as much as they are able to grasp. In fact I never speak to people in any other way. I do this to fulfill what God said through the prophet: "I will speak to them in parables; I will tell them things unknown since the foundation of the world."

Privately, however, I explained everything to my disciples. *(Matt. 13:34–35; Mark 4:33–34)*

What the Parable of the Weeds Means

After telling these parables to those gathered outdoors, I went inside where my disciples asked me to explain the parable of the weeds.

I said, "The man who sowed the good seed is the Son of Man. The field is the world; the good seed are the people who belong to the kingdom, and the weeds are those who belong to the evil one. The enemy who sowed the weeds is the devil, the harvest is the close of the age, and the reapers are the angels. Just as weeds are gathered up and burned in the fire, so will it be at the end of time. The Son of Man will send out his angels to gather from his kingdom everything that traps people into sin as well as the sinners themselves. The angels will throw them into the blazing furnace where there will be weeping and gnashing of teeth. Then the upright will shine like the sun in the kingdom of their Father. Anyone who is willing to listen should listen." *(Matt. 13:36–43)*

The Parables of the Hidden Treasure and of the Pearl

"The kingdom of heaven is also like a treasure which a man found hidden in a field. Delighted with his good fortune, he covers up the treasure, goes and sells everything he owns, then comes back and buys the field.

"Again the kingdom of heaven is like a man in search of fine pearls. When he finds one of unusual value, he goes out and sells everything he owns so he can buy it." *(Matt. 13:44–46)*

THE PARABLE OF THE NET

"The kingdom of heaven is like a large net that fishermen cast into the sea to catch fish of every kind. When the net is full, they pull it ashore and separate the catch; good fish are put into baskets, and poor fish are thrown away. This is what it will be like at the end of the age. The angels will come and separate the wicked from the upright, then throw the wicked into the blazing furnace where there will be weeping and gnashing of teeth." *(Matt. 13:47–50)*

GEMS OF TRUTH

I asked those who had been listening to me, "Do you understand these parable I have told you?"

"Yes," they answered, "we do."

Then I said to them, "So everyone who knows the law and is trained for the kingdom of heaven is like a rich man who brings from his storehouse gems of truth both old and new." *(Matt. 13:51–52)*

Chapter Thirteen

MINISTRY IN JERUSALEM AND THE DEATH OF JOHN THE BAPTIST

HEALING AT THE POOL OF BETHESDA

Some time later I went up to Jerusalem to take part in one of the Jewish festivals. Near the sheep gate was a pool, which in Hebrew was called Bethesda. It had five covered porches where a number of invalids used to lie—the blind, the lame, and others withered by disease.

One man lying there had been an invalid for much of his life. When I heard that he had been in that condition for thirty-eight years, I asked him, "Would you like to get well?"

In a sorrowful voice he answered, "Sir, I don't have anyone to put me in the pool when the water begins to stir. So while I'm trying to get to the pool, someone else always gets there first."

I said to him, "Stand up! Pick up your mat and start walking!" The man was healed instantly. He stood, picked up his mat, and started to walk.

This happened on a Sabbath day, so the Jewish authorities said to the man who had just been healed, "You shouldn't do that! Carrying a mat on the Sabbath is against the Law."

"But the man who made me well told me to pick it up and walk," he replied.

"Who told you that?" they asked. "Who told you to pick up your mat and walk?" The man didn't know my name, and by then I had slipped away into the crowd.

Later on as I was walking in the temple area, I met the man I had healed. "Now that you are well again," I said, "don't go on sinning or something worse may happen to you." Once he knew who it was who had healed him, the man went to the Jewish authorities and told them.

Because I kept doing things like this on the Sabbath, the Jewish authorities began increasingly to harass me. I said to them, "Since my Father continues to do his work, I am free to do my work as well." That made them try all the harder to get rid of me. They held that not only was I breaking the Sabbath, but, by referring to God as my Father, I was claiming equality with God.

"I tell you the truth; I, the Son, can do nothing on my own initiative. I can do only what I see my Father doing. Whatever my Father does, I do. The Father loves me and shows me all that he himself is doing. And greater works than these will he show me so that you may be filled with wonder. Just as the Father raises the dead and gives them life, so also do I give life to those I choose.

"The Father himself passes judgment on no one but has made me, the Son, the judge of all. Therefore everyone should honor me as much as they honor him. To withhold honor from me is to dishonor the Father who sent me. I tell you the truth, the one who listens to my message and believes in the one who sent me has eternal life already. He is no longer headed toward judgment but has moved from the realm of death into life.

"I tell you the truth, the time will come—in fact, it is already here—when those who are spiritually dead will hear my voice; and if they pay attention to it, they will live. The Father himself is the source of all life and has allowed me the same privilege. He has given me the authority to act as judge because I am the Son of Man.

"Don't be surprised at this because the time is coming when all the dead will hear my voice and come out of their graves. Those who have lived a good life will rise to life eternal, but those who have lived a sinful life will rise to face judgment.

"I can do nothing on my own initiative. I judge only as God tells me, and this judgment is fair because I seek his will, not my own pleasure.

"If I testify on my own behalf, you have no way of knowing if it is true. There is, however, someone who speaks on my behalf, and I know that what he says about me is true. You sent messengers to John the Baptist, and what he said about me was true. Of course, I don't need someone else to validate my claims, but I tell you this so you may be saved. John was a lamp, burning and giving light. And for a time, you were willing to rejoice in the light he provided.

"But I have greater evidence than the words of John—specifically, the miraculous deeds that I do. They were assigned to me by the Father, and they prove conclusively that I was sent by the Father.

"You search the Scriptures because you think that in them you will find eternal life. These same Scriptures speak about me, but you refuse to come to me and receive life.

"I am not looking for your praise; I know that you have no real love for God in your hearts. I have come as a representative of my Father, and you won't accept me. But when others come as their own spokesmen, you will accept them. How can you ever believe if you are seeking the praise of one another rather than the praise that comes from God?

"Don't think that I will be the one to accuse you before the Father. Moses will be your accuser, the one on whom you have set your hope. If you really believed Moses, you would believe me because it was about me that he wrote. But if you don't believe what he wrote about me, how can you believe the claims I make?" *(John 5:1-47)*

OPINIONS ABOUT ME

When Herod, the ruler of Galilee, heard the reports about me and what I was doing, he was thoroughly confused. Some people told him that I was actually John the Baptist risen from the dead. (That would explain the miraculous powers working through me.) Others claimed that I was Elijah who had reappeared and still others that I was one of the ancient prophets come back to life.

"How could this man be John the Baptist," reasoned Herod, "since I had him beheaded? Perhaps he was raised from the dead." So Herod kept trying to see me. *(Matt. 14:1-2; Mark 6:14-16; Luke 9:7-9)*

THE DEATH OF JOHN THE BAPTIST

Herod had arrested John, chained him up, and thrown him in prison. He did it as a favor to Herodias, his brother Philip's wife whom he had married. John had repeatedly told Herod, "It is not lawful for you to be living with your brother's wife." So Herodias was furious with John. She wanted to get him out of the way but couldn't manage it. Herod knew that John was a good and holy man. Since he had a certain respect for him, he provided protection. He would have liked to have had him executed but was afraid of the people who believed him to be a prophet. Besides, Herod liked to listen to what John had to say, although it usually left him perplexed.

One year when Herod decided to celebrate his birthday with a lavish banquet, Herodias saw her chance. Herod invited all the nobles of his court, his military commanders, and the leading citizens of Galilee. On that festive occasion the daughter of his wife Herodias danced for the gathering. Everyone was delighted so Herod told her, "You may ask me for anything you want, and I will give it to you." He even sealed the promise with an oath, "Whatever you ask for, I will give it to you, up to half of my kingdom."

So she went to her mother and asked, "What should I ask for?"

"The head of John the Baptizer," demanded Herodias.

The daughter hurried back to Herod and said, "What I want is the head of John the Baptizer. I want it on a tray, and I want it right now."

King Herod was filled with remorse but could hardly refuse her because of the vow he had made in the presence of his guests. So he sent an executioner to the prison to behead John and bring his head back on a tray. The order was carried out, and John's head was brought to the daughter on a tray. She in turn gave it to her mother. When John's disciples learned what had happened, they came and took his body and laid it in a tomb. *(Matt. 14:3–12; Mark 6:17–29)*

FIVE THOUSAND ARE FED

About that time the apostles returned from their missionary trip and presented me with a detailed report of everything that had happened. The days were so full that they hardly had enough time to eat.

Obviously they were tired so I encouraged them to join me in a quiet place where they could rest. We left by boat to a remote area near Bethsaida. People from the nearby villages saw the boat as it set sailed and knew that my disciples and I were aboard. So they ran along the shore and arrived ahead of us. When I stepped from the boat, I was met by a huge crowd of people, and my heart went out to them. They were like sheep without a shepherd. So I began to teach them about God's great kingdom and to heal all who were sick.

As the day wore on, my disciples came to me saying, "This is a desolate spot, and the hour is late. Let the crowd go to the nearby villages where they can buy food and find a place to stay."

But I said to them, "No, it is up to you to give them something to eat."

"How could we possibly do that?" they asked. "It would take at least two hundred silver coins worth of bread to feed this many people, and we don't have the money."

"Well, how much bread do you have? Go and take a look."

They came back and reported, "We have only five loaves of bread and two fish."

So I told them to have the crowd sit down on the green grass in groups of fifty and a hundred. Then I took the five loaves and the two fish, raised my eyes to heaven, and gave thanks to God. I broke the bread and began handing the pieces to the disciples to distribute among the people. I also divided the two fish. Every last person in the crowd ate to his heart's content. Then the disciples picked up what was left over and filled twelve baskets with the scraps. There were five thousand men who ate that day plus all the women and children. *(Matt. 14:13–21; Mark 6:32–44; Luke 9:10–17)*

WALKING ON THE WATER

When evening came, I told my disciples to get into the boat and cross to the other shore. I would stay behind to tell the crowd we were leaving. After sending the disciples away, I went up the hillside by myself to pray. Evening came, and by now the boat was three or four miles from shore. A strong head wind had risen, and the boat was taking a severe beating. At daybreak I came walking toward them on top of the waves. When they saw me, they were terrified and shrieked for fear, "It's a ghost!"

I responded quickly, saying, "All is well! It is I. You don't need to be afraid."

Peter asked, "Lord, if it is really you, then tell me to come to you across the water."

"It is I, Peter. You may come."

So Peter stepped out of the boat and started to walk across the water. However, when he noticed how strong the wind was, he panicked. That was when he started to sink. "Lord!" he cried, "save me!"

Instantly I reached out my hand and took hold of him. "What little faith you have, Peter! What made you lose your confidence?" As soon as we got into the boat, the wind died down, and all was still. The passengers in the boat bowed before me, exclaiming, "You are indeed the Son of God."

The disciples still did not understand the real meaning of the feeding of the five thousand; their minds were closed. In a short time we were near Capernaum. *(Matt. 14:22–33; Mark 6:45–52; John 6:16–21)*

HEALING AT GENNESARET

We came to land at Gennesaret where we tied up the boat. As I was getting out, people immediately recognized me. They hurried all over the countryside and brought the sick on stretchers. And wherever I went—in villages, towns, or the countryside—they brought their sick to the marketplace and begged me to let the sick just touch the fringe of my cloak. As many as touched it were restored to perfect health.

The next morning, back across the lake, the crowds discovered that I was no longer with them. They knew that I had not gone with the disciples. Fortunately, some boats from Tiberias had drifted ashore near the place where the five thousand had been fed. The people crowded into these boats and came across the lake to Capernaum looking for me. When they found me there on the other side of the lake, they asked, "Rabbi, how did you get here, and when?" *(Matt. 14:34–36; Mark 6:53–56; John 6:22–25)*

Chapter Fourteen

THE BREAD OF LIFE DISCOURSE AND PETER'S GREAT CONFESSION

THE BREAD OF LIFE

"I tell you the truth," I said to those who had followed me to Capernaum, "you've been trying to find me not because you saw the miracles I did but because I gave you all you wanted to eat. Do not work for the food that is here today and gone tomorrow but for the food that produces eternal life. I, the Son of Man, will give you this food because I am the one authorized by God the Father."

"What is it," they asked me, "that God wants us to be doing?"

I answered, "What God requires is that you believe in me, the one he has sent."

They asked, "What miraculous sign are you going to do so that, when we see it, we will believe in you? What will it be? For example, our ancestors were given manna to eat in the desert. As Scripture says, 'Moses gave them bread from heaven to eat.'"

"I tell you the truth," I said, "it was not Moses who gave you bread from heaven; it is my Father who is giving you the true bread from heaven. I am the bread of God that came down from heaven and gives life to the world."

The people said, "Sir, give us this bread now and never stop!"

"I am the bread of life," I responded. "No one who comes to me will ever be hungry again. No one who believes in me will ever be thirsty again. As I told you before, although you have seen me, you still do not believe. Everyone the Father has given me will come to me, and I will not reject any of you.

"I came down from heaven not to do my own will but the will of the one who sent me. His will is that not a single one of those he gave me will be lost but that on the last day every one of them will be raised to eternal life. He wants everyone who sees the Son to believe in me and have eternal life. Then on the last day I will raise them up."

Then the crowd began to complain because I said, "I am the bread that came down from heaven." They asked, "But aren't you the son of Joseph, the carpenter? Don't we know your father and mother? So how can you say that you came down from heaven?"

I replied, "Stop grumbling among yourselves. No one can come to me unless the Father draws him. And whoever does come, I will raise to eternal life on the last day. One of the prophets wrote, 'They will all be taught by God.' So everyone who listens to the Father and learns from him will come to me.

"Of course, I am the only one who has seen the Father because I came from his presence. I alone have seen the Father. I tell you the truth, everyone who believes in me has eternal life.

"I am the bread of life. Your ancestors ate manna in the desert, yet in time they all died. But now the true bread has come down from heaven, and whoever eats it will never die. I am the living bread, come down from heaven. Whoever eats this bread will live forever. This bread is my flesh that I give to bring life to the world."

These words led to a heated argument among the crowd. "How is it possible for this man to give us his flesh to eat?" they asked.

"I tell you the truth," I said, "unless you eat the flesh of the Son of man and drink his blood, you will not have eternal life. But if you do eat my flesh and drink my blood, you will have eternal life, and I will raise you up on the last day. My flesh is the real food, and my blood is the real drink. Whoever eats my flesh and drinks my blood sustains a personal relationship with me, and I with him.

"The Father of life sent me, and I have life because of him. In the same way, the one who eats me will have life because of me. The bread that came down from heaven is not like that which your ancestors ate. They died, but whoever eats this bread will live forever."

I taught all these things in the synagogue at Capernaum. *(John 6:26–59)*

DEFILEMENT—TRADITIONAL AND REAL

One day some Pharisees and legal experts came down from Jerusalem to hear what I had to say. They noticed that some of my disciples were eating with unclean hands, that is, hands that had not been ritually cleansed. (The Pharisees, and all other Jews for that matter, do not eat unless they wash their hands in the way prescribed by tradition. They do not eat anything from the marketplace unless it is first cleansed. This is one of the many traditions they cling to; another is the ceremonial cleansing of cups, pots, and copper bowls.)

The religious fundamentalists from Jerusalem put this question to me, "Why don't your disciples live according to the tradition of the elders? Why do they eat with defiled hands?"

I answered, "Isaiah was right when he prophesied about you hypocrites. As it is written: 'This people honor me with their lips, but their hearts are far from me; they worship me in vain, teaching human ideas as though they were divine truth. You have substituted the teachings of men for the truth of God.'

"You have a clever way of rejecting the law of God in order to uphold your own teaching. For example, Moses said, 'Honor your father and your mother'; and, 'Whoever speaks evil of his father or mother must be put to death.' But you teach that if someone tells his parents, 'Whatever help you might have expected from me is Korban' (that is, "dedicated to God"), then he is no longer permitted to help them. In this way you invalidate the Word of God for the sake of your own tradition. And this is but one of the many examples of how you replace God's truth with human tradition."

Then I invited the crowd to come closer (they had moved away, perhaps out of respect for the "intelligentsia") and said to them, "Listen to me, all of you, and understand what I say. There is nothing that goes into you from without that can defile you. Rather it's what comes out of you that makes you unclean."

When I had dismissed the people and gone indoors, my disciples asked me to explain what I had just said. "Are you as dull as all the others?" I asked. "Don't you understand that what a person eats cannot defile him because it doesn't go into his heart but into his stomach, and from there it is discharged into the sewer (thus declaring all foods fit to be eaten). What defiles a person is what comes out from within. From man's heart come evil ideas, sexual immorality, theft, murder, adultery, greed, evil, deceit, indecency, envy, slander, pride, and folly. All of these things come from without and defile." *(Matt. 15:1-20; Mark 7:1-23)*

THE SYROPHOENICIAN WOMAN

I left Galilee and traveled north into the area around the cities of Tyre and Sidon. I didn't want anyone to know where I was staying, but I soon found out I couldn't keep it a secret. Right away a Greek woman, a Syrophoenician by birth, heard that I was there and came, crying out, "Lord, Son of David, have mercy on me! My daughter is in terrible trouble; a demon has taken control of her." I gave her no answer, not a single word.

The disciples came and begged me to do something about it. "Send her away," they said. "She keeps following us wherever we go, making a terrible racket."

So I said to the woman, "I was sent to help the lost sheep of the House of Israel and no one else."

But the woman paid no attention to my words. Falling at my feet, she begged, "Lord, please help me! Drive the evil spirit out of my daughter!"

I said to her, "First I must feed my children, the Jews. They come before anyone else. It wouldn't be fair to take their bread and throw it to the dogs, the Gentiles."

"That's true, Lord," she countered, "but even dogs get to eat the scraps that fall from their master's table."

I couldn't help but acknowledge, "You are a woman of remarkable faith. May it be done for you as you wish. You can go back home now, for the demon has left your daughter."

And at that moment her child was healed. When she arrived home, she found her daughter lying in bed freed from the evil spirit. *(Matt. 15:21–28; Mark 7:24–30)*

I Heal a Deaf Mute and Many Others

Then I left the region of Tyre and went by way of Sidon to the Sea of Galilee in the region of the Decapolis (the Ten Towns). I went up into the hill country around the lake and sat down to teach. Great crowds followed me, bringing the lame, the blind, the crippled, those unable to speak, and many others. They placed them at my feet, and I cured them all.

One such person was a deaf man with a speech impediment. His friends brought him to me and begged me to lay my hands on him and heal him. I took the man away from the crowd so the two of us could be alone. I put my fingers into his ears, then touched his tongue with spittle. Looking up into heaven, I gave a deep sigh and said, "Ephphatha!" (which means, "Be opened"). Immediately the man's ears were opened, and he could hear; his speech impediment was removed, and he could talk without any trouble.

I ordered the crowd not to tell anyone about what had happened, but the more I insisted, the more they spread the news. People were completely amazed and exclaimed, "How perfectly he does everything! He actually makes the deaf hear and the dumb speak." And they praised the God of Israel. *(Matt. 15:29–31; Mark 7:31–37)*

Four Thousand Are Fed

Not long after that, a great crowd gathered and had nothing to eat. So I called the disciples together and said, "I am sorry for all these people because they have been with me now for three days and have nothing left to eat. If I send them away hungry, they may collapse along the way, for some of them have come a long distance."

The disciples replied, "But where in this desolate place can we find enough to feed so many?"

"How many loaves do you have?" I asked.

"Seven," was the answer.

"What about fish?" I added.

"Well, we do have a couple of fish, but they're hardly big enough to eat."

I told the crowd to sit down on the ground. Then I took the seven loaves and the fish, gave thanks to God, and broke the bread into pieces. I gave the bread and the fish to the disciples, who distributed them to the hungry crowd. Every last person ate all he wanted, and when the disciples collected the scraps, they were able to fill seven baskets with the leftovers. Four thousand men ate that day, and that's not counting the women and children.

After encouraging the people to return home, I got into a boat and crossed over to the region of Magadan, or Dalmnutha. *(Matt. 15:32–39; Mark 8:1–10)*

THE PHARISEES SEEK A SIGN

One day some of the Pharisees and Sadducees came to me asking to see a miracle. They were testing me to see whether my claims were legitimate. I said to them, "When evening comes, you look at the sky and declare, 'Tomorrow the weather will be good because, look, the sky is red!' But if the sky is red in the morning, you say, 'Looks like we'll have a storm today; the sky is threatening.' When you see a cloud bank in the west, you say, 'There'll be a rainstorm'—and sure enough, before long, it begins to rain. When a south wind begins to blow, you say, 'It'll be a hot one today,'—and that's what happens. You hypocrites, you know how to predict the weather by looking at the sky, but you have no idea how to interpret the times you live in."

Then I gave a deep sigh of indignation and said, "How is it that you are unable to grasp the significance of my presence in your midst? You are an evil and apostate generation, asking me to prove myself with some miraculous sign; but no sign will be given to you except the sign of Jonah." With that I left and set sail toward the eastern shore of the lake. *(Matt. 16:1–4; Mark 8:11–13; Luke 12:54–56)*

THE YEAST OF THE PHARISEES

The disciples had forgotten to bring enough bread, and we had only one loaf there in the boat. "Be on watch," I warned, them. "Have nothing to do with the yeast of the Pharisees and the Sadducees or the yeast of Herod."

The disciples began to discuss among themselves what I had said, thinking that I was talking about their failure to bring bread. So I said to them, "You men have so little faith! Why are you discussing your lack of bread? Do you still not see or understand? Are your minds so dull? You have eyes; can't you see? You have ears; can't you hear? You remember, don't you, when I broke the five loaves and fed five thousand men? When you picked up the scraps, how many baskets did you fill?"

"Twelve," they answered.

"And when I broke the seven loaves and fed the four thousand, how many baskets of scraps did you pick up?"

"Seven," they answered.

"Doesn't that mean anything to you?" I said. "How could you think I was talking about the bread we eat? What I said was, 'Beware of the yeast of the Pharisees and Sadducees.'"

Then the disciples began to catch on that it wasn't the yeast in bread I was warning them about, but the "yeast" [the deceptive teaching] of the Pharisees and the Sadducees. *(Matt. 16:5–12; Mark 8:14–21)*

A BLIND MAN IS HEALED AT BETHSAIDA

When we arrived at Bethsaida, some people brought a blind man to me and begged me simply to touch him. I took the blind man by the hand and led him outside the village. Then, moistening his eyes with spittle, I laid my hands on him and asked, "Now can you see anything?"

The man, whose sight was beginning to come back, replied, "Well, I can see people, but they look like trees walking around."

So I laid my hands on his eyes a second time. This time the man's vision came into focus, and his sight was completely restored. For the first time he could see everything clearly and distinctly. I sent him directly home, telling him not to stop at any village along the way. *(Mark 8:22–26)*

MANY DISCIPLES TAKE OFFENSE AT ME

Many of my followers who had been listening said, "This teaching is offensive; who can accept it?"

I knew that they were grumbling about it, so I said, "Does this shock you? Then what would you think if you were to see me, the Son of Man, return to heaven where I came from? It is the Spirit who gives life; human nature is of no help. The words that I have spoken to you are from that life-giving Spirit. But some of you do not believe." (From the beginning I knew who wouldn't believe in me. I also knew who would betray me.)

I added, "That's why I told you, 'No one can come to me unless the Father makes it possible.'"

As a result, many of my followers turned their backs on me and no longer followed me. *(John 6:60–66)*

PETER'S CONFESSION

I turned to my disciples and asked, "You're not going to leave me like they did, are you?"

Simon Peter answered, "Lord, to whom would we go? You are the one whose words give eternal life. We are convinced that you are the Holy One of God."

I replied, "Did I not choose all twelve of you? Yet one of you is the devil." I was talking about Judas, the son of Simon Iscariot. Although Judas was one of the twelve disciples, before long he would betray me.

Continuing along the way with my disciples, I entered the district of Caesarea Philippi. One day while we were alone, I was praying. I asked my disciples, "What do people say about the Son of man? Who do they say I am?"

They answered, "Some say you're John the Baptist; others say Elijah; and still others, that you are Jeremiah or some other ancient prophet risen from the dead."

"But what about you?" I asked. "Who do you say I am?"

Speaking for the Twelve, Simon Peter answered, "You are the promised Messiah, the Son of the living God."

"You are highly favored, Simon son of Jonah, because you didn't learn that from some human source; it was revealed to you by my Father who is in heaven. And I say to you, 'You are Peter, the Rock; and on this rock I will build my church. Not even the powers of the underworld can hold out against it. I will give you the keys of the kingdom of heaven. Whatever you rule out on earth will be ruled out in heaven, and whatever you allow on earth will be allowed in heaven.'"

Then I ordered the disciples to tell no one that I was the promised Messiah. *(Matt. 16:13–20; Mark 8:27–30; Luke 9:18–21; John 6:67–71)*

I Foretell My Passion

Now for the first time I began to say plainly to my disciples, "It is necessary that I go to Jerusalem and suffer at the hands of the elders, the chief priests, and the scribes. They will put me to death, but after three days I will rise again to life."

Peter took me aside and began to correct me. "God forbid it, Lord," he said, "this must never happen to you!"

I turned, and facing my disciples, said to Peter, "Get out of my sight, you Satan! You are an obstacle in my way because you look at everything from a human standpoint, not as God sees it." *(Matt. 16:21–23; Mark 8:31–33; Luke 9:22)*

"If Any Man Would Come after Me . . ."

Then, calling the crowd to join the disciples, I said to them all, "If anyone wants to be my disciple, he must put his own interests aside, take up his cross, and follow me from that point on. The one who tries to save his life [get as much as possible for himself out of this life] will certainly lose it; but the one who loses his life [surrenders it in service to me and the good news] will be rewarded with a full and abundant life. After all, what good would it be to gain the whole world if, in the bargain, you had to forfeit your own life? There is no way to buy back a life once it is lost.

"If anyone is ashamed of acknowledging me in this apostate and sinful age, I, the Son of Man, will be ashamed of him when I come back in the glory of my Father accompanied by holy angels. At that time each person will be rewarded for what he has done. I tell you the truth, there are some standing right here who will not experience death until they see me returning to rule as king." *(Matt. 16:24–28; Mark 8:34–9:1; Luke 9:23–27)*

Chapter Fifteen

THE TRANSFIGURATION AND SUBSEQUENT TEACHING

THE TRANSFIGURATION

About a week later I took Peter and the brothers James and John up a high mountain where we could be alone. While I was praying, my face began to shine like the sun, and my clothes turned a dazzling white, as white as white could be. Suddenly Moses and Elijah appeared in glorious splendor and began to talk with me about my approaching death and resurrection, a destiny I would soon fulfill in Jerusalem.

Peter, James, and John had grown sleepy, but when they saw this glorious scene, they became wide awake. Then, as Moses and Elijah began to leave, Peter blurted out, "Master, it is wonderful for us to be here! If you want me to, I will set up three shrines, one for you, one for Moses, and one for Elijah." He was so overwhelmed that he simply said the first thing that came to mind.

While Peter was still speaking, a luminous cloud appeared and covered them with its shadow. From within the cloud came a voice, saying, "This is my Son whom I love, the Chosen One. Pay attention to what he has to say."

When the three disciples heard this, they fell to the ground, overcome by fear. I stepped forward and touched them, saying, "Stand to your feet; don't be afraid." Looking up, they saw that Moses and Elijah were no longer there. The disciples kept this to themselves and told no one what they had seen. *(Matt. 17:1–9; Mark 9:2–10; Luke 9:28–36)*

THE COMING OF ELIJAH

As we left the place of transfiguration, I told the three disciples (Peter, James, and John) to tell no one what they had seen until I had been raised from the dead. So they didn't tell anyone about what had happened on the mountaintop, although they did question one another as to what "rising from the dead" could possibly mean. The disciples asked me, "Why do the rabbis say that Elijah must come before the promised Messiah?"

I answered, "Elijah will in fact come first and put everything in order. But I tell you that Elijah has already come, and they didn't recognize him. Instead they did to him whatever they wanted to do. In the same way, the Son of Man is now about to suffer at their hands and be treated with contempt." Then the disciples understood that I was speaking about John the Baptist. *(Matt. 17:10–13; Mark 9:11–13)*

I HEAL A BOY WITH AN EVIL SPIRIT

On the following day, after we had come down from the mountain, we saw the disciples surrounded by a large crowd. They were arguing with the scribes. When the crowd realized that it was I, they were greatly excited and ran at once to welcome me.

I asked, "What's the argument all about?"

A man from the crowd stepped forward and knelt before me. "Teacher," he said, "I beg you to have mercy on my son, my only child. He is an epileptic and under the control of an evil spirit, which renders him speechless. Whenever this wicked spirit seizes him, he screams and goes into convulsions, foaming at the mouth and grinding his teeth. Sometimes he goes rigid. He suffers terribly, and the evil spirit simply will not leave him alone. I brought the boy to your disciples and begged them to cast out the demon, but they weren't able to do it."

I couldn't help but say to the crowd, "You unbelieving and misguided generation! How much longer must I be with you? How much longer must I put up with you? Bring me the boy."

So they brought him to me. Immediately the evil spirit threw the boy into convulsions. He fell to the ground and lay there writhing, foaming at the mouth.

"How long has this been going on?" I asked.

"Ever since he was a little boy," the father replied. "The demon has often tried to destroy him by throwing him into fire or into water. If you can do anything, please have compassion on us and help us."

"'If you can?'" I queried. "Everything is possible for the one who believes."

"I do believe!" cried out the father, "Help me to overcome my unbelief!"

When I saw that people were crowding around to see what was happening, I rebuked the evil spirit: "You dumb and deaf spirit, I command you to come out of this boy! You may never enter him again!" The demon shrieked, threw the boy into another convulsion, and left. The boy looked like a corpse, and most of the crowd believed him to be dead. But I took him by the hand and raised him to his feet. Instantly he was healed and able to stand by himself. Then I presented him to his father, and the crowd was astonished at this mighty act of God.

When we had gone indoors, away from the crowd, my disciples asked, "Why couldn't we cast out the demon?"

"You couldn't do it because you didn't have enough faith," I answered. "I tell you the truth, if you have faith even the size of a mustard seed and say to a mountain, 'Move from here to there,' it will obey you. If you have faith, nothing will be impossible. Only by prayer can an evil spirit like this be driven out." *(Matt. 17:14–21; Mark 9:14–29; Luke 9:37–43a)*

I FORETELL MY PASSION AGAIN

As we continued our journey through Galilee, the crowds marveled at everything I was doing. But I wanted it to be kept a secret. I said to my disciples, "Listen carefully to what I have to say, and think it over. The Son of Man will be betrayed into the hands of his enemies, and they will kill me. But three days after my execution, I will come back to life." The disciples were baffled by what I was telling them, but they were afraid to ask me to explain what it all meant. They were unable to grasp the meaning of what I was saying, for it was concealed from them. *(Matt. 17:22–23; Mark 9:30–32; Luke 9:43b–45)*

WHO PAYS THE TEMPLE TAX?

When we arrived in Capernaum, the tax collectors came to Peter and asked, "Doesn't your teacher pay the half-shekel temple tax?"

"Of course he does," said Peter.

Peter then entered the house and was about to bring up the subject when I said, "What do you think, Simon? Where do earthly kings get their tolls and taxes? From their own sons or from strangers?"

Peter answered, "From strangers, of course."

"Well then," I continued, "their sons are exempt, are they not? But we don't want to leave the impression that we have no regard for the temple, so go down to the lake and drop in a line. Take the first fish you catch, open its mouth, and there you will find a large silver coin. Take it and give it to them to pay our taxes." *(Matt. 17:24–27)*

WHO'S THE GREATEST?

On the way to Capernaum, the disciples had been arguing among themselves about who would be the most important in the kingdom of heaven. I knew what they were thinking, so when we arrived in town and had gone inside, I asked, "What were you discussing along the way?"

Embarrassed by the question, they remained silent.

So I sat down to teach them an important lesson in humility and true greatness. "The heart of the issue," I said, "is that anyone who would be first must first of all become last, the servant of all."

Calling a child into the circle, I took the little one into my arms and said, "Unless you receive the kingdom of God like this child, you will never enter it. You must change your ways and become like children if you want to enter my kingdom. Along the way you were wondering who is the greatest in the kingdom of heaven, and the answer is: the one who humbles himself like this child. Whoever receives one like this in my name receives not only me but the one who sent me. So the one who is truly great is the one who is least among you." *(Matt. 18:1–5; Mark 9:33–37; Luke 9:46–48)*

THE STRANGE EXORCIST

Then John said to me, "Master, we saw a man using your name to drive out demons, and we tried to stop him because he wasn't one of us."

"You shouldn't do that," I said, "for no one who uses my name to perform a miracle will be able soon afterward to say something evil about me. Whoever is not against us is for us. I assure you that if someone gives you a cup of water to drink because you belong to me, he will by no means lose his reward." *(Mark 9:38–41; Luke 9:49–50)*

ENTICING OTHERS TO SIN IS A SERIOUS MATTER

Then I taught my disciples that if anyone should cause one of my humble followers to sin, it would be better for that person to have had a large millstone tied around his neck and been thrown into the open sea to drown. Woe to the world for its enticements to sin! Temptations are inevitable, but woe to the one through whom they come!

"If your hand causes you to sin, cut it off. It would be better for you to enter the life to come with only one hand than to have two and be thrown into the eternal fire. If your foot causes you into sin, cut it off. It would be better for you to enter the life to come with only one foot than to have two and be thrown into the unquenchable fire of hell. And if your eye causes you to sin, gouge it out and throw it away. It would better for you to enter the coming life with only one eye than to have two and be thrown into the flames

of hell where the maggots never die and the fire never goes out."
(Matt. 18:6–9; Mark 9:42–50; Luke 17:1–3a)

ON REPROVING ONE'S BROTHER

"If a fellow believer does something wrong against you, rebuke
him; go to him in private and lay before him the offense. If he listens
and repents, then forgive him—you have won back your brother. If
he refuses to hear you out, then go to him again, but this time take
along several members of the congregation so that, as Scripture
says, the matter may be examined by two or more witnesses. If he
refuses to listen to them, then report the problem to the church;
and if he won't pay attention to them, then treat him as a pagan or
a tax collector.

"I tell you the truth, whatever you prohibit on earth will be pro-
hibited in heaven, and whatever you allow on earth will be allowed
in heaven." *(Matt. 18:15–18; Luke 17:3)*

"WHERE TWO OR THREE ARE GATHERED . . ."

"I want you to know that if two of you here on earth agree
in prayer about something, my Father in heaven will be sure to
answer.

"Wherever two or three of you gather to worship, I will be right
there with you." *(Matt. 18:19–20)*

ON RECONCILIATION

Then Peter came to me and asked, "Lord, how many times must
I forgive a fellow believer who keeps sinning against me? As many
as seven times each day?" [The rabbinic view was three.]

"Not merely seven times," I answered, "but if he comes saying, 'I repent,' you must forgive him seventy times seven." *(Matt. 18:21–22; Luke 17:4)*

THE PARABLE OF THE UNFORGIVING SERVANT

"The kingdom of heaven may be compared to a king who decided to review how well his palace staff had done with the finances entrusted to them. It was determined that the first manager owed the king ten thousand talents. Since he could not pay off such a huge debt, the king ordered him to be sold as a slave, along with his wife, his children, and everything he owned. The proceeds would be applied toward the debt. Hearing this verdict, the manager fell to his knees begging the king, 'Be patient with me, and I will pay back all I owe.' The king felt sorry for him, cancelled the debt, and let him go.

"Upon leaving the king, this manager ran into a fellow manager who owed him a hundred silver coins. Grabbing him by the throat and nearly choking him, he demanded, 'Pay back all you owe me!'

"This unlucky colleague fell at his feet begging, 'Be patient with me, and I will pay you back.' But he wouldn't agree; instead he had the poor man jailed until he could pay back the debt in full.

"When the other managers of the royal court learned what had happened, they were filled with indignation. They went to their master and related the injustice. Then the king sent for the first manager and denounced him, saying, "You scoundrel! When you begged me, I cancelled your entire debt, and it was considerable. Were you not obligated, then, to have mercy on your colleague, just as I had mercy on you?' So in his anger the king had the man tortured until he should pay back the entire amount that he owed."

Then I concluded, "That is how my heavenly Father will deal with you unless you forgive your fellow believer from your heart." *(Matt. 18:23–35)*

Chapter Sixteen

HEADING TOWARD JERUSALEM

DEPARTURE TO JUDEA

Now when the time drew near for me to be taken up to heaven, I set out for Jerusalem determined to carry out my role. I sent messengers on ahead to a Samaritan village to make preparations. However, the people there would not receive me because it was clear to them that I was determined to go to Jerusalem. When my disciples James and John heard about this, they said, "Lord, do you want us to call down fire from heaven and reduce them to ashes?"

But I turned and rebuked them. Then we went on to a different village. *(Matt. 19:1–2; Mark 10:1; Luke 9:51–56)*

ON FOLLOWING ME

As we were walking along the road, a legal expert said to me, "Teacher, I will follow you no matter where you go."

I reminded him, "Foxes have dens and wild birds have places to roost, but I have nowhere to lie down and rest, a place I can call my own."

To another man, I said, "Follow me."

But he said, "Lord, let me take care of my father during his declining days. Then when he is gone I will follow you."

I told him, "Let the dead bury their own dead. As for you, go and spread the good news of the kingdom of God."

Yet another said, "I will follow you, Lord; but let me first go and say good-bye to my family."

I answered, "The person who starts to plow but keeps looking back is not fit for the kingdom of God." *(Matt. 8:18–22; Luke 9:57–62)*

COMMISSIONING THE SEVENTY

After this I appointed seventy-two disciples (apart from the Twelve) and sent them on ahead of me two by two into every place I planned to visit. I said to them, "Many people are ready for the kingdom so the harvest is great, but the workers are few. So ask the Lord, to whom the harvest belongs, to send out workers into the fields to bring in the grain. Be on your way! I am sending you out like sheep in the midst of a pack of wolves. Leave your money belt at home. And you won't need to take a traveling bag or an extra pair of sandals. Don't stop to greet anyone along the way.

"Whenever you enter someone's house, your first words are to be, 'May the peace of God be on this house.' If a man of peace lives there, your blessing will remain on him; but if not, it will return to you. Stay there, eating and drinking whatever they provide, for the worker deserves his pay. Don't keep moving from one house to another.

"When you enter a town and the people welcome you, eat what they place before you, heal the sick, and tell them, 'The kingdom of God has drawn near.' But should you enter a town that will not welcome you, go out in its streets and say, 'Even the dust of your town that sticks to our feet we wipe off in protest against you. But remember this: the kingdom of God has drawn near you.' Believe me when I say that on the Day of Judgment, God will show more mercy to Sodom than to that town." *(Luke 10:1–12)*

"HE WHO HEARS YOU, HEARS ME . . ."

Then I said to my disciples, "Whoever listens to you is listening to me; whoever rejects what you have to say is rejecting me; and whoever rejects me is rejecting God, the one who sent me." *(Luke 10:16)*

THE RETURN OF THE SEVENTY

The seventy-two disciples came back jubilant from their mission trip. "Lord," they exclaimed, "even the demons submitted to us when we spoke in your name."

"Yes," I told them, "I was watching as God cast Satan out of heaven like a flash of lightening. And now you understand that I have given you power to crush the opposition represented by a hostile creation (snakes and scorpions) and to overcome the power of the enemy, Satan. Nothing can hurt you. Nevertheless, don't rejoice because the forces of evil obey you, but rejoice that your names are registered in heaven." *(Luke 10:17–20)*

THE PARABLE OF THE GOOD SAMARITAN

One day a legal expert was anxious to justify himself, so he posed the question, "Just who is my neighbor?"

To answer his question I told him this parable:

"A man on his way down from Jerusalem to Jericho was attacked by a band of ruffians. They ripped off his clothes, beat him half to death, and left him lying beside the road. A priest happened to be going down the same way, and when he came to the victim, he crossed to the other side of the road. So also, a Levite, when he came by, glanced at the man lying there, then crossed the road and continued on. But a Samaritan who was traveling that way, when he saw the injured man, was moved with compassion. He went to him, poured oil and wine on his wounds, and bandaged them. Then he lifted the man onto his own donkey and took him to an inn where he took care of him. On the following day when he left, he took out two silver coins and gave them to the innkeeper saying, 'Take care of him, and when I come back this way, I will make good any additional expense you may have incurred.'

"Now which of those three do you think proved himself a neighbor to the man who fell into the hands of thugs?" I asked.

"The one who showed him mercy," the lawyer answered.

So I said, "Then go and live like that." *(Luke 10:29–37)*

MARY AND MARTHA

As we continued on our way, we came to a village where a woman named Martha invited me into her home. She had a sister, Mary, who settled down at my feet and listened to what I was saying. Martha, on the other hand, became upset with the responsibilities of serving. She broke into the room where we were gathered, saying, "Lord, don't you care that my sister has left me to prepare and serve dinner all by myself? Speak to her so she will come and do her share."

I answered, "Martha, dear Martha, you worry and fret about so many things while only one thing is really important. What

Mary has chosen is the best, and it will not be taken from her."
(Luke 10:38–42)

THE LORD'S PRAYER

One day I had just finished a time of prayer when one of my
disciples said to me, "Lord, teach us to pray, just as John the Baptist
taught his disciples."

So I told them that when they prayed they should say:

> Father,
> May your name be held in honor,
> May your kingdom come.
> Give us every day the bread we need for that day,
> And forgive us our sins as we ourselves have forgiven
>   those who have sinned against us.
> Keep us from trials we can't handle. *(Luke 11:1–4)*

THE MIDNIGHT CALLER

Then I said to them, "Suppose one of you has a friend and you
go to him in the middle of the night and say, 'Please lend me three
loaves of bread because a friend of mine has showed up and I have
nothing for him to eat.'

"And suppose your friend inside the house yells back, 'Don't
bother me. The door is already locked for the night, and my children are here in bed with me. I'm in no condition to get up and give
you anything.'

"What then? I tell you that even though the man in bed with his
children won't get up and help you out because of friendship, if you

keep knocking long enough, he'll be forced to get up and give you what you want." *(Luke 11:5–8)*

ENCOURAGEMENT TO PRAY

"Ask, and God will give to you; search, and you will find; knock, and the door will be opened to you. For the one who keeps on asking receives, and the one who searches diligently finds, and the one who won't stop knocking will have the door opened to him.

"I'm sure that no father among you, should his son ask for a fish would hand him a snake; or should he ask for an egg would give him a scorpion. So if you, corrupt as you are, know how to give good things to your children, how much more will your heavenly Father give the Holy Spirit to those who ask." *(Luke 11:9–13)*

TRUE BLESSEDNESS

While I was speaking, a woman in the crowd shouted out, "May God bless the womb from which you came, and the breasts which nursed you."

I responded, "Rather, may God bless those who hear the word of God and put it into practice." *(Luke 11:27–28)*

CONCERNING LIGHT

"You don't light a lamp and then put it under a basket or hide it in the cellar. You put it on a lamp stand so every one in the house can see." *(Luke 11:33)*

THE SOUND EYE

"The eye is like a lamp for the body. It follows that if your eye is clear it will allow the entire body to be filled with light. But if your eye is cloudy, your whole body will be dark. Think again about the light you believe you have; it could be darkness." *(Luke 11:34–36)*

DISCOURSE AGAINST THE PHARISEES AND LAWYERS

When I had finished speaking, a Pharisee invited me to come and dine with him. So I went to his house and sat down to eat. The Pharisee was surprised that I didn't wash my hands before eating (as Jewish custom requires). So I said to him, "You Pharisees clean the outside of the cup and dish, but inside you are full of extortion and wickedness. You fools! Did not God, who made the outside, make the inside as well? So give from your heart to the poor, and everything will be clean for you.

"But woe to you Pharisees! For you tithe the income from your garden herbs, such as mint and rue, but you neglect justice and love for God. You should do the former but not neglect the more important.

"Woe to you, Pharisees! For you like to take the seats of honor in the synagogues and to be greeted with respect in the market-place. Woe to you! You are like unmarked graves which pollute those who step on them without realizing it."

One of the legal experts said to me, "Teacher, when you say things like that about the Pharisees, you also insult us."

I responded, "Woe to you legal experts as well. You load people with burdens too heavy to carry, yet you yourselves are unwilling to lift even a finger by way of help. Woe to you! You build memorial tombs for the prophets, the very ones your ancestors killed. In this way you show that you approve of what your ancestors did; they murdered the prophets, and you built their tombs. For this reason God in his wisdom said, 'I will send them prophets and apostles, some of whom they will kill; others they will persecute.' So the people of this generation will have to answer for the blood of all the prophets shed since the world was created, from the blood of Abel to the blood of Zechariah, who was killed between the altar and the holy place. Yes, I tell you, this generation will have to answer for them all. Woe to you legal experts! You have removed the key from the house of knowledge. Not only have you yourselves never entered that house, but you have stood in the way of others who would like to enter."

After saying these things, the religious authorities became even more hostile. They followed along after asking me innumerable questions about many things, hoping to trap me in something I might say. *(Luke 11:37–54)*

THE YEAST OF THE PHARISEES

Meanwhile, the crowd had grown so large that thousands were pressing together, and some were being trampled. I spoke, first of all, to my disciples, saying, "Be on guard against the yeast of the Pharisees, that is, their hypocrisy." *(Luke 12:1)*

Chapter Seventeen

TEACHING EN ROUTE TO JERUSALEM

THE HELP OF THE HOLY SPIRIT

"Whoever speaks against the Son of Man can be forgiven, but whoever persistently rejects the Holy Spirit can never be forgiven.

"And when they bring you to trial in the synagogues, before rulers and authorities, don't worry about what you should say or how you might defend yourself. When the time comes, the Holy Spirit will make clear to you the right thing to say." *(Luke 12:10–12)*

WARNING AGAINST GREED

One day a man in the crowd shouted out, "Teacher, make my brother share the family inheritance with me!"

I refused, saying, "My good man, no one has appointed me to act as judge or arbitrator of personal disputes. Be careful! You need to be on guard against greed of every kind; for true life is not determined by what a person has, even when he has far more than he needs." *(Luke 12:13–15)*

The Parable of the Rich Fool

To drive home this point, I told them this parable:

"Once there was a rich man whose land was very productive. He reasoned with himself, saying: 'What should I do? I don't have enough space to hold the crop about to be harvested. Oh, I know what I'll do; I'll tear down my barns and build bigger ones. Then I'll have plenty of room to store all my grain and the other crops as well. I can say to myself, "You lucky man! You've stored up ample goods for years to come. Now you can take it easy. Eat! drink! And enjoy yourself!"'

"But God said to him, 'You fool! This very night the angels are coming for your soul. Once you're dead, who will get everything you've stashed away for yourself?'"

I concluded, "This is how it will turn out for those who have stored up treasure for themselves instead of becoming rich toward God." *(Luke 12:16–21)*

Anxiety about Earthly Things

Then I turned to my disciples and said, "That's why I tell you to stop worrying about such menial things as whether you will have enough food to eat or clothes to wear. Certainly there is more to life than food and clothing.

"Think for a moment about the ravens. They neither plant the seeds, harvest the crop, or store the grain in barns; yet God continues to provide them what they need. Think about it! Are you not of far greater value than the birds? Furthermore, which of you by worrying can add even a single moment to his life? If you can't manage a little thing like that, why waste your time worrying about bigger things?

"Look at the wild flowers out in the fields, how they grow. They are not hard at work making their own clothing, yet I can assure you that not even Solomon dressed in his royal robes could match the beauty of one of these. Now if God clothes the fields with such beautiful flowers, which today are in bloom but tomorrow wither away, is he not much more likely to clothe you? How reluctant you are to trust him! Don't be overly concerned about what to eat or drink; stop worrying about such incidentals. Unbelievers are the ones who make food and drink a major concern in life, but in your case your heavenly Father already knows you need such things, and he will take care of it.

"Instead, make the kingdom of God your central concern, and God will provide whatever you may need. There is no need to be afraid, little flock, for the Father delights in giving you the blessings of his kingdom." *(Luke 12:22–32)*

TREASURES IN HEAVEN

"Sell what you have and give the proceeds to those in need. The purse that holds your treasure should be a heavenly purse. That kind doesn't wear out with time, a thief can't steal it, and the moth can't eat holes in it—your treasure remains safe. The important point is that wherever you store your treasure, that is where your heart will be." *(Luke 12:33–34)*

WATCHFULNESS AND FAITHFULNESS

"The Lord will return at an hour you least expect, so get ready for that great day. Keep your lamps burning. Be like servants waiting for their master's return from a wedding party; they stand ready at a moment's notice to throw open the door when he knocks.

Blessed are those servants whose master finds them alert and ready for his return! I tell you the truth, the master himself will prepare to serve them; he will seat them at the table and wait on them. How blessed are those he finds ready, even though he comes late at night or even after that.

"You may be sure that if the owner of the house had known at what hour of the night the burglar would come, he would have stayed awake and kept him from breaking in. You too must always be ready, for the Son of Man will come when you least expect him."

Then Peter asked, "Lord, is that parable intended only for us or for everyone?"

I answered, "Who then is a faithful and wise steward? Is he not the one the master will put in charge while he is gone so that the other servants will get their fair share of food at the proper time? Blessed is that steward who is faithfully carrying out his responsibility when his master returns. I tell you the truth, the master will put him in charge of everything he owns.

"But if that wicked steward should reason, 'My master has delayed his coming,' and begins to beat the other servants, both men and women, and to eat, drink, and get drunk. Then when the master returns without notice, he will flog him severely and assign him the fate of the unfaithful and the hypocrite, where there is weeping and gnashing of teeth.

"The servant who knows what his master wants but doesn't get ready and do it will receive a severe beating. But the servant who does not know what his master wants and does what deserves punishment will receive a light whipping. Much is required of the one to whom much is given; and of the one who has been entrusted with much, a great deal will be required." *(Luke 12:35–48; Matt. 24:45–51)*

AGREEMENT WITH ONE'S ACCUSER

"And why don't you judge for yourselves what is right? For example, if someone brings a lawsuit against you, do your best to settle the dispute before it gets to court. Otherwise, when your opponent drags you before the judge, the judge may decide against you and turn you over to a guard who will put you in prison. There you will remain—count on it!—until you have paid the last single penny of your debt." *(Luke 12:57–59)*

THE PARABLE OF THE BARREN FIG TREE

On that occasion I was told that Pilate had massacred some Galileans as they were offering their sacrifices at the altar. I asked them, "Do you think those Galileans were worse sinners than the others because they suffered in that particular way? No indeed! And I tell you that unless you turn from your sins, you will all perish just as miserable a death. Or what about those eighteen people who were killed when the tower in Siloam fell on them? Do you think that proves they were worse sinners than anyone else in Jerusalem? No indeed! And I tell you that unless you turn from your sins, you will all perish just as miserable a death."

Then I told them this parable:

"Once there was a man who had a fig tree growing in his yard. Every time he came expecting to find fruit, he found none. So he said to the worker in charge, 'For three years now I have come expecting to find fruit on this fig tree, and so far, not a single fig. Cut it down! Why should it use up good soil?'

"'Sir,' replied the worker, 'can't we give it one more year? I'll put some manure around the tree and dig it in. Maybe by harvest it will produce figs. If not, then go ahead and cut it down.'" *(Luke 13:1–9)*

THE HEALING OF THE WOMAN ON THE SABBATH

One Sabbath day I was teaching in a synagogue, and a woman was there who for eighteen years had not been able to stand up straight, crippled as she was by an evil spirit. When I saw her, I called her over and said, "Woman, I am going to set you free from your deplorable condition." Then I touched her, and instantly she stood straight up and began to praise God. The leader of the synagogue was indignant that I had performed this healing on the Sabbath. To the crowd he said, "There are six days in every week in which work can be done; people ought to come on one of those days if they want to be cured, but never on the Sabbath."

"You hypocrites!" I retorted, "Every one of you is guilty because there isn't one of you who wouldn't untie his ox or donkey and lead it out to water just because it was the Sabbath. Shouldn't this woman, a daughter of Abraham, whom Satan kept in bonds for eighteen years, be set free, even on the Sabbath?"

This answer embarrassed my opponents, but the crowd was overjoyed at all the wonderful things I was doing. *(Luke 13:10–17)*

EXCLUSION FROM THE KINGDOM

I continued going through towns and villages, always teaching, as I pressed on toward Jerusalem. Along the way someone asked, "Lord, will only a few be saved?"

I answered, "Do your utmost to enter through the narrow door, for many, I tell you, will try to get in but not be able. Once the master of the house has gotten up and locked the door, you may find yourself standing outside pounding on the door and begging, 'Please Lord, unlock the door so we can come in.'

"And he will say, 'I don't know you or where you come from.'

"Then you will answer, 'One time, when you were in our town teaching, we shared a meal with you.'

"The master will respond, 'I know nothing of you or where you come from? Get out of my sight, all you wicked people!' How you will wail and grind your teeth when you see Abraham, Isaac, and Jacob, plus all the prophets in the kingdom of God while you are excluded.

"At that time people will come from east and west, from north and south, and take their places at the great messianic banquet in the kingdom of God. And note: some guests who at one time seemed so unimportant are now in the choice seats, and some you expected to see at the speaker's table are way back in the corner." *(Luke 13:22–30)*

A WARNING AGAINST HEROD

Just then some Pharisees came up and warned me to leave because Herod Antipas was laying plans to kill me. I told them, "Go and tell that fox that for the time being I intend to continue my work of casting out demons and healing the sick; after that I will go to Jerusalem and complete my mission. Indeed, in spite of Herod's plans to harm me, I must continue my journey to Jerusalem because, as you have heard it said, 'It is impossible for a prophet to die outside of Jerusalem.'" *(Luke 13:31–33)*

HEALING THE MAN WITH DROPSY

One Sabbath I was invited to dinner at the house of a prominent Pharisee. Right there in front of me was a man whose body was swollen with fluid, so of course, the people were watching me closely to see what I would do. Since a number of experts in religious law were there, I posed this question to them: "Does our law allow us to heal on the Sabbath or not?" They wouldn't answer, so I took hold of the man, healed him, and sent him away. Then I said to them, "Which one of you, if his son or his ox should fall into a water hole, would not, right then and there, pull him out even though it was the Sabbath?" Once again they had no answer. *(Luke 14:1–6)*

TEACHING ON HUMILITY

Another day, this time at a wedding feast, I couldn't help but notice how the guests were scrambling for the best possible seats. So I gave them this advice:

"When someone invites you to a wedding feast, don't take the seat of honor. A person more distinguished than you may also have been invited, and the host will have to come and say to you, 'You are sitting in this man's seat. Please move.' Then, to your embarrassment, you will have to go down to the foot of the table. Instead, when you arrive, take a seat of less importance so that when your host finds you there he will say, 'Move up, my friend. We have a better seat for you.' This way you will be honored in the presence of all the guests. As I have said before, everyone who exalts himself will be humbled; the one who humbles himself will be exalted."

Then I said to the one who invited me, "When you host a lunch or a dinner, don't invite your friends or your brothers, or even your relatives or rich neighbors. It follows that they will invite you back, and in this way you will be repaid for what you did. When you host a party, invite the poor, the crippled, the lame, and the blind. Then you will be blessed because they don't have any way to repay you; God will take care of that on the day when upright people rise again." *(Luke 14:7–14)*

THE PARABLE OF THE GREAT SUPPER

Upon hearing this, one of the dinner guests exclaimed to me, "What a privilege to be invited to a banquet in the kingdom of God!"

I told him this parable:

"Once there was a man who planned a lavish dinner party and sent out many invitations. As the time drew near, he sent his servant to tell the guests that everything was ready. They, however, without exception began to make excuses.

"The first one said, 'I've just bought some land and must go and inspect it. Please accept my apologies.'

"Another said, 'I've just bought five pair of oxen, and I'm on my way to try them out. Please accept my apologies.'

"Still another said, 'I've just gotten married, so obviously I won't be able to come.'

"So the servant returned and reported this to his master. The master of the house was furious. He said to the servant, 'Hurry out into the streets and back lanes of the city and bring back the poor, the crippled, the blind, and the lame.'

"Upon returning, the servant reported, 'Sir, I have done as you ordered, and there is still room.'

"So the master said, 'Go out onto the country lanes and hedgerows and urge people to come in so that my house will be full. For I tell you that not a single one of those who were invited at first will share in my banquet.'" *(Luke 14:15–24)*

Chapter Eighteen

MORE PARABLES AND TEACHING

THE COST OF DISCIPLESHIP

Wherever I went, large crowds followed me. On one occasion I said to them, "Whoever would be my disciple must care more for me than for his own father or mother, his wife or his children, his brothers or his sisters, yes, even his own life. And whoever does not carry his own cross and live as I live, cannot be a disciple of mine. Tell me: if you want to build a tower, don't you first sit down and calculate the cost? Otherwise you may not have the resources to complete it. Once the foundation is laid and you don't have enough money to go any farther, everyone who sees it will ridicule you. They'll say, 'There's the man who started to build a tower but couldn't complete the job.'

"Or what king, who intends to go to war, doesn't sit down first and determine whether, with his ten thousand soldiers, he can defeat an army twice that size? If he can't, then, while the enemy is still a long way off, he will send a delegation to discuss terms of peace.

"In the same way," I concluded, "if you want to become a disciple of mine, you'll have to give up everything you call your own." *(Luke 14:25–33)*

THE PARABLE OF SALT

"Salt is good, but if it gets stale, it can't be made salty again. Since it is of no use for either the soil or the manure pile, it is thrown away. Whoever has ears to hear had better pay attention." *(Luke 14:34–35)*

THE PARABLE OF THE LOST SHEEP

"Be careful not to look down on one of the little ones with contempt, for in heaven their angels have uninterrupted access to the Father."

Among those who regularly came to hear what I had to say were a number of tax collectors in addition to people of no particular religious persuasion. The Pharisees and professional clerics began to grumble among themselves, saying, "This man makes friends with common people; he even eats his meals with them!"

So I told them this story:

"Which one of you, if you had a hundred sheep and one strayed away, would not leave the ninety-nine in the desert pasture and go in search of the one that was lost? When you found it, you would hoist it onto your shoulders and carry it back home. Then you would call your friends and neighbors and exclaim, 'Come and rejoice with me; I have found the sheep that was lost!' In the same way there will be more joy in heaven over one sinner who repents than over ninety-nine respectable people who haven't strayed away." *(Matt. 18:10–14; Luke 15:1–7)*

THE PARABLE OF THE LOST COIN

"Or again, what woman, should she lose one of her ten silver coins, would not light a lamp and sweep the house looking in every corner until she found it? Then when she found it, she would call her friends and neighbors and exclaim, 'Rejoice with me; I have found the coin I lost.' In the same way there is rejoicing among the angels of God over one sinner who repents." *(Luke 15:8–10)*

THE PARABLE OF THE PRODIGAL SON

I went on to tell them this parable:

"There was once a man who had two sons. The younger one said to his father, 'Father, I don't want to wait until you die to receive my share of the estate. Please give it to me now.' So the father divided all he had between the two sons.

"A few days later the younger son turned his share into cash and left home for a distant country. Once there he squandered his fortune in wild and reckless living. It so happened that when he had spent all he had, a terrible famine fell on the land, and he found himself facing starvation. So he hired out to one of the local landowners who sent him out to his farm to take care of pigs. The young man got so hungry that he would gladly have eaten his fill of the bean pods the pigs ate, but no one would let him have any.

"Finally he came to his senses. He asked himself, 'How many of my father's hired hands have all they need to eat and then some, and here am I, dying of hunger! I will leave this wretched place and go back to my father and confess, "Father, I have sinned against God and against you. No longer do I deserve to be called your son; please take me on as one of your hired hands."'

"So the prodigal son left the distant land and headed back home. While he was still at a distance, his father saw him, and his heart was moved with compassion. He ran out to his son, threw his arms around him, and kissed him. The boy cried, 'Father, I have sinned against God and against you. No longer do I deserve to be called your son.'

"But the father ordered his servants, 'Hurry, bring out the best robe and throw it around his shoulders; put a ring on his finger and sandals on his feet. Then go get the calf we have been fattening and kill it. We're going to celebrate with a feast! I thought this son of mine was dead, but here he is, alive. I thought I'd lost him for good, but he's been found.'

"And so they began to celebrate.

"Meanwhile, the older son was out in the fields. On his way in from work, he passed near the farmhouse and heard all the music and dancing. 'What in the world is that all about?' he asked one of the servants.

"'Your brother is back!' exclaimed the servant. 'Your father has killed the prize calf because his son is back home safe and sound.'

"The older son was so angry that he wouldn't go in the house. So the father went out and begged him to come in and take part in the celebration. The older son burst out, 'All these years I have slaved for you and never refused to do anything you told me. And what did I get out of it? You've never given me so much as a young goat so I could celebrate with my friends. But when this son of yours turns up—the one who squandered your wealth on women of the street—you go and kill the choice calf in his honor.'

"Then the father said to him, 'My dear son, you have always stayed here with me, and everything I have is already yours. But there is good reason to celebrate this joyful day—your brother was dead but now has come back to life; he was lost but now has been found.'" *(Luke 15:11–32)*

THE PARABLE OF THE UNJUST STEWARD

Here is another story I told my disciples.

"Once there was a rich man whose property manager was accused of wasting his master's assets. So he called him in and said, 'Why do I hear these accusations about you? Turn in a record of all your financial dealings so I can find out what has been going on. You may no longer serve as my property manager.'

"The servant thought to himself, 'Now that my master is removing me from this position, what can I possibly do? I'm not strong enough to labor in the field, and I'm too proud to beg. Ah, I know what to do so that when I'm no longer in this position friends will still welcome me into their homes.'

"So one by one he called in those who were leasing land from his master. To the first he asked, 'How much do you pay my employer for the land you lease?'

"The man answered, 'One hundred barrels of olive oil per year.'

"'Here is the agreement. Sit right down and change it to fifty barrels.'"

"Then to another he asked, 'And you, how much do you have to pay?'

"'A hundred containers of wheat,' answered the second man.

"'Here is the agreement. Take it and change it to eighty.'

"Upon learning of these adjustments [made possible, perhaps, by dropping interest or personal commission], the rich man had to applaud what his knavish steward did to ensure his own future. For the people of this world are more shrewd in dealing with their own kind than the people who belong to the light.

"So my counsel to you," I advised, "is to make friends for yourself by a generous use of your earthly possessions so that when they are gone God will welcome you into your eternal home." *(Luke 16:1–9)*

BEING FAITHFUL IN LITTLE THINGS

"The one who proves trustworthy in little things will also be trustworthy in more important matters. And whoever cheats when it doesn't matter will also cheat when it does. So if you haven't been trustworthy in handling worldly wealth, how can you be trusted with the true wealth of heaven. And if you haven't been trustworthy in this life with what God has given, how can he trust you with more in the life to come?" *(Luke 16:10–12)*

ON SERVING TWO MASTERS

"No servant can be the slave of two masters, for either he will hate the one and love the other or be loyal to one and despise the other. You simply cannot serve both God and money at the same time." *(Luke 16:13)*

THE PHARISEES REBUKED

When the Pharisees heard all that I was saying about wealth, they began to ridicule me because they were fond of their money. I said to them, "You people are the very ones who pass yourselves off as righteous in men's eyes. But God can read your hearts, and what the world holds in high esteem is loathsome in the sight of God." *(Luke 16:14–15)*

CONCERNING THE LAW

"Up until the time of John the Baptist, the Law of Moses and the writings of the prophets were in effect. Since then, the kingdom of God has been proclaimed and all are urged to enter it. The Law, however, hasn't been discarded. It would be easier for heaven and earth to pass away than for a single stroke of the Law to disappear." *(Matt. 11:12–13; 5:18; Luke 16:16–17)*

CONCERNING DIVORCE

"Any man who divorces his wife and marries another woman is living in adultery, and the man who marries the divorced woman is also living in adultery." *(Luke 16:18)*

THE PARABLE OF THE RICH MAN AND LAZARUS

"Once there was a rich man who dressed in the most expensive clothes (elegant purple robes and linen underneath). Every day he feasted sumptuously, while at his door lay a poor beggar whose body was covered with sores. This beggar, Lazarus, longed to satisfy his hunger with scraps that fell from the rich man's table, but the only satisfaction he got was that the dogs came and licked his sores.

"In the course of time, the beggar died and was carried away by angels to sit next to Abraham at the great feast in heaven. The rich man also died and was buried. In Hades, where he was being tormented, he looked up and saw Abraham in the distance with Lazarus by his side. He cried out, 'Father Abraham, have mercy on me! Tell Lazarus to dip the tip of his finger in water and come and cool my tongue, for I am in terrible anguish here in these flames.'

"But Abraham said, 'Remember, my son, that in your lifetime you had your fill of good things, just as Lazarus had his fill of bad. But now he is being comforted, and you are in anguish. Besides that, God has established a great chasm between the departed, so that in spite of what one might wish, no one can cross in either direction.'

"So the rich man said, 'Then I beg you, Father Abraham, send Lazarus to my father's house because I have five brothers who need to be warned so they won't end up here with me in this place of torment.'

"'Your brothers have Moses and the prophets to warn them,' answered Abraham; 'Let them listen to what they have to say.'

"'But that is not enough, Father Abraham,' said the rich man. 'If someone would rise from the dead and go to my brothers, then I know they would turn from their sinful ways.'

"'No,' said Abraham, 'if they won't listen to Moses and the prophets, they won't be convinced even though a person should rise from the grave and deliver a firsthand report.'" *(Luke 16:19–31)*

THE SERVANT'S RESPONSIBILITY

"Do any of you ever say to a servant just in from plowing a field or herding sheep, 'Come on in and have dinner with me.' Don't you rather say to the servant, 'Prepare my supper, then get ready and serve me while I enjoy my evening meal. Then when I'm done, you can prepare your own meal.' Is the master indebted to a servant who did only what was required of him? Certainly not.

"It is the same with you; when you have done all you were told to do, you should say, 'We deserve no special praise, for we are simply servants who have done what was expected of us.'" *(Luke 17:7–10)*

TEN LEPERS CLEANSED

On my way to Jerusalem, I passed through the border region between Samaria and Galilee. There I entered a village and was met by ten men with leprosy. Keeping their distance, they called out, "Jesus! Master! Have pity on us!" I looked at them and said, "Go to the priests and let them examine you."

As they were on their way, the leprosy vanished. One of the ten, realizing that he was cured, rushed back to where I was waiting, praising God at the top of his voice. Falling facedown at my feet, he thanked me again and again for what I had done. (This man was a Samaritan.)

"Where are the other nine?" I asked those who were standing by. "Has only this one man returned to give praise to God? And he's not even a Jew." Then I said to the man at my feet, "Stand up now, and be on your way; your faith has healed you." *(Luke 17:11–19)*

THE COMING OF THE KINGDOM OF GOD

One day some Pharisees asked me when the kingdom of God would come. I answered, "The kingdom of God doesn't come with signs from heaven, nor will someone say, 'Look, here it is!' or 'There it is!' for the reign of God is already active in your midst." *(Luke 17:20–21)*

THE DAY OF THE SON OF MAN

Then I said to my disciples, "The time will come when you will long to see the glorious reign of the Son of Man, but my time has not yet come. People will tell you, 'Look, there he is!' or, 'Look, over there!' But don't rush out to track me down. For when I return, it will be like lightning flashing across the sky. However, before that happens, I must suffer many things and be rejected by my contemporaries. As it was in the time of Noah, so will it be when I return. People were busy eating and drinking, marrying and giving their children in marriage, until the day when Noah went aboard the ark and the flood came and destroyed all the rest. It will be just as it was in the days of Lot; people were eating and drinking, buying and selling, planting and building. But on the day Lot left Sodom, fire and brimstone came raining down from heaven and destroyed them all. That is how it will be on the day the Son of Man is revealed. But until then everything will continue as it is.

"Whoever happens to be on top of his house when I return will not have time to come down and pack his belongings. If someone is out in the fields, he shouldn't try to make it back to the house. Remember what happened to Lot's wife when she looked back! [She turned into a pillar of salt!] So whoever tries to make his life secure will lose it, but whoever is ready to lose his life will preserve it. On that fateful night two will be lying on one bed; one will be taken and the other left. Two women will be grinding corn together; one will be taken and the other left."

At this point the disciples broke in, "Lord, where will this take place?"

I answered, "It will be as unmistakable as vultures hovering over a dead body." *(Luke 17:22–37)*

THE PARABLE OF THE UNJUST JUDGE

I wanted to encourage my disciples to pray at all times and never give up so I told them the following parable:

"Once in a certain city there was a fiercely independent judge who paid no attention to the laws of God or to public opinion. In the same city was a widow who kept coming to him, pleading for justice against an opponent. For a long time the judge tried to ignore her, but finally he said to himself, 'Even though I'm free to do what I choose in this case—I'm under no obligation to anyone—I'm going to see that justice is done for this widow because she is pestering me to death and before long will wear me out with her incessant pleas.'"

Then I said to my disciples, "If a judge devoid of compassion answered the widow's pleas in that way, just think what a righteous God will do for his own people who cry out to him day and night in prayer? Will he not vindicate them even though he seems to delay? I promise you, he will see that justice is done and done speedily. Nevertheless, when the Son of Man returns, will I find those who believe enough to pray?" *(Luke 18:1–8)*

THE PHARISEE AND THE PUBLICAN

I told this next parable to those who were sure of their religious superiority and looked down on every one else:

"Two men went to the temple to pray: one a Pharisee, the other a tax collector. The Pharisee chose a prominent spot and began to pray about himself, saying, 'I thank you, God, that I am not like other people, greedy, dishonest, sexually immoral, and especially like that tax collector over there. I go without food twice a week, and I give you a tenth of all my income.'

"The other man stood off to one side and would not even raise his eyes to heaven but beat his breast in despair and prayed, 'O God, be merciful to me, a sinner!'"

Then I concluded: "I tell you, it was the tax collector, not the Pharisee, who went home freed from guilt. For those who exalt themselves will be humbled, but those who humble themselves will be exalted." *(Luke 18:9–14)*

Chapter Nineteen

THE FEAST OF TABERNACLES IN JERUSALEM

I REMAIN IN GALILEE

The Jewish authorities in Judea were determined to kill me, so I remained where I was in Galilee and continued my ministry. The time for the Jewish festival of Shelters was approaching, so my brothers said to me, "You ought not stay here in Galilee; go to Judea so that your followers will be able to see the miraculous things you are doing. No one acts in secret if he wants to become well known. Since you can do such miraculous things, let the whole world know about it." (Even my own brothers did not believe in me).

I replied, "My time has not yet come, but your time is always here. People hate me because I tell them that what they are doing is evil, but you give people no reason to hate you. Go on up to the festival. I won't be going there right now because the right time for me has not yet come." So I stayed behind in Galilee. *(John 7:1–9)*

To Jerusalem Secretly

However, after my brothers left for the festival, I did go up to Jerusalem, not with the others but by myself.

The Jewish leaders were expecting me at the festival. They kept asking, "Has anyone seen him yet?" There was a lot of guarded discussion about me among the crowds. While some held me to be an honorable man, others said that I was deceiving the common people. But since the people were afraid of their leaders, no one spoke openly against me. *(John 10:10–13)*

Teaching in the Temple

About midway through the festival, I went into the temple courts and began to teach. The Jewish leaders were astonished when they heard me. They asked, "How come this man knows so much when he hasn't studied under our rabbis?"

"What you hear me teaching is not something I made up," I said. "It comes from the one who sent me. If a person chooses to obey God, he will know that what I am teaching comes from God. I am not speaking on my own. Whoever speaks on his own authority wants to bring honor to himself. But the one who desires to bring honor to the one who sent him is a person of integrity; there is nothing fraudulent about him. It was Moses, was it not, who gave you the law? But none of you are keeping it. Otherwise you wouldn't be trying to kill me."

The crowd shot back, "A demon has driven you mad! What makes you think someone is trying to kill you?"

I answered, "I performed a miracle on the Sabbath, and you were all offended by it. Moses ordered you to circumcise your sons (actually the practice began with the patriarchs, not Moses), so you go ahead and circumcise even if the required time falls on the Sabbath. If you can circumcise on the Sabbath without breaking the law of Moses, why are you upset with me because I made a man completely well on the Sabbath? Stop judging on such a superficial level. Get to the heart of the matter."

Then some who lived in Jerusalem said, "Isn't this the man they want to put to death? Yet here he is, speaking in public, and no one has said a word to stop him! You don't suppose the authorities have come to accept him as the Messiah? No, that couldn't be! No one knows where the Messiah will come from, and everyone knows that Jesus is from Nazareth."

At that I raised my voice and spoke out clearly, "So you think you know me and where I came from, do you? The truth is that I didn't come on my own initiative but was sent by God. He is the one who sent me. You don't know him, but I know him because I came from him."

Some of the people were anxious to arrest me, but no one laid a hand on me because my time had not yet come. However, many in the crowd believed in me. They reasoned, "When the Messiah comes, he surely won't do more miracles than this man has done."

When the Pharisees learned that the crowd was seriously considering whether I might be the Messiah, they got together with the chief priests and sent temple guards to arrest me.

I told the people, "I will be with you a little while longer, and then I will return to the one who sent me. You'll look for me, but you won't find me. Where I am, you cannot come."

The Jewish authorities said to one another, "Where does he think he could go that we couldn't find him? He can't possibly think that by going to some foreign country and continuing his teaching among people there, he could escape us! What did he mean when he said, 'You will look for me, but you won't find me,' and, 'Where I am you cannot come?'"

On the last and most important day of the festival, I stood up and spoke in a loud voice so all could hear, "If you are thirsty, come to me and drink. If you believe in me, rivers of living water will flow from deep within you, just as the Scripture says." I was speaking of the Holy Spirit who would be given to every believer. The Spirit had not yet been given because I had not yet been raised to glory. *(John 7:14–39)*

DIVISION AMONG THE PEOPLE

When the people heard these words, some said, "Without a doubt this man is the prophet!"

Others said, "No, he is the Messiah."

Still others argued, "Surely the Messiah is not to come from Galilee. Scripture says that the Messiah will be a descendant of King David and be born in Bethlehem, the village where David lived." So the people had various ideas as to what should be done with me. Some wanted to arrest me right there on the spot, but no one laid a hand on me.

When the temple guards went back to the chief priests and Pharisees, they were asked, "Why didn't you bring him with you?"

"No one has ever spoken like that man!" they declared. "Don't tell me that you too have been fooled," said the Pharisees. "Note that none of the chief priests or Pharisees have fallen for him. As for this mob that knows nothing of the law, they're all headed for hell anyway!"

Nicodemus (who had met with me at an earlier time) was one of this group. He asked the others, "Is it not true that according to our law a man cannot be condemned until he's had a chance to answer the charge?"

His colleagues responded scornfully, "Are you also from Galilee? Search the Scriptures, and you will see for yourself that no prophet ever comes from Galilee." *(John 7:40–52)*

THE WOMAN CAUGHT IN ADULTERY

As it was getting late, everyone left for home, but I went to the Mount of Olives. Early the next morning I returned to the temple courts. The people soon gathered, so I sat down [as the rabbis do] and began to teach them.

The legal experts and the Pharisees brought me a woman who had been caught in the act of adultery. They made her stand where everyone could watch and said to me, "Teacher, this woman was caught in the act of adultery. The law of Moses tells us to put a woman like this to death by stoning. What do you say?" [The question was posed as a trap. They intended to use my answer as a basis for bringing charges against me.]

Rather than giving them an answer, I bent over and started writing on the ground with my finger.

So they kept pressing the question about the woman. Finally I straightened up and said, "The one without sin among you should be the first to throw a stone at her." Then I bent over and started writing again. When they heard this, they began to slip away one by one, beginning with the oldest. Finally the woman and I were there alone.

"Woman," I asked, "where did they all go? Is there no one left to accuse you?"

"No one, sir," she replied.

Then I said, "Neither am I going to accuse you. You may leave, but from now you are not to continue in your sinful ways." *(John 7:53–8:11)*

"I AM THE LIGHT OF THE WORLD"

Once again I addressed the Pharisees. I said, "I am the light of the world. Follow me and you won't stumble along in the dark. You will have the light that leads to life."

The Pharisees protested, "You are testifying on your own behalf, so anything you say about yourself is not valid."

I answered, "Even if I do testify on my own behalf, what I say is valid because I know where I came from and where I am going. But you haven't the slightest idea of my origin or my destiny. Your judgment is superficial, but I pass judgment on no one. However, if I did pass judgment, my verdict would be trustworthy because I am not alone when I judge; the Father who sent me is with me. According to your own law there must be two witnesses before something is acknowledged as true. I am one of the witnesses, and my Father who sent me is the other!"

"And where is this 'Father' of yours?" they asked.

I replied, "You haven't the slightest idea as to who I am or who my Father is! If you knew me, you would know my Father as well."

I taught these truths in the temple precincts, near the place where the offerings were collected. But no one arrested me because my time had not yet come. *(John 8:12–20)*

DISCUSSION WITH THE JEWS

So I went on to tell them, "I'm going away, and you can't go where I am going. You'll try to find me, but you will die in your sins."

The Jewish leaders mocked, "Perhaps he intends to kill himself and end up in Hades. That would explain why we can't go where he is going!"

"You are from below," I replied; "I am from above. You belong to this world; I do not. That's why I told you that you will die in your sins. For if you don't believe that I am who I say I am, you will die with your sins unforgiven."

Caustically they responded, "Just who do you think you are?"

"I am who I told you from the beginning," I answered. "I could say a lot more to condemn you, but the Father who sent me is reliable. I say nothing but what I have heard from him." (I was implying that God was my Father, but they didn't catch on.)

I said to them, "When you lift me up on the cross, then you will know that I am who I say I am. I do nothing on my own and speak only those things the Father has taught me. The one who sent me is with me. He has not abandoned me because I always do what pleases him." *(John 8:21–29)*

"THE TRUTH WILL SET YOU FREE"

Many who heard me say these things came to believe in me. So I said to the Jews who believed, "If you let what I say control every aspect of your life, you will demonstrate that you really are my disciples. You will come to know the truth, and the truth will set you free."

"But we are descendants of Abraham," they boasted. "We have never been in bondage to anyone! How can you say, 'You will be set free'?"

Jesus answered, "I tell you the truth, everyone who keeps on sinning is a slave to sin. A slave does not remain permanently in the home, but a son remains forever. So if the Son sets you free, you will be free indeed." *(John 8:30–36)*

CHILDREN OF THE DEVIL

"I know that you belong to the lineage of Abraham. But you are trying to kill me anyway. My teaching has not changed your heart. I am telling you the things my Father has shown me; just as you are doing what your father has taught you."

"Abraham is our father!" they claimed in anger.

I quietly asserted, "If you were Abraham's children, you would be conducting yourselves as Abraham did. Instead you are bent on killing me for telling you the truth that I heard from God. Abraham would never have done anything like that! You are doing what your father does."

"We were not born out of wedlock!" they jeered. "We have one father—God!"

"If God were your father," I said, "you would love me because I came from God to be with you. He is the one who sent me. I didn't come on my own. Why can't you understand what I am saying? The answer is that even before you hear me you are convinced that I am wrong. Your father is the devil, and you like to please him. From the beginning he has been a murderer and a liar. There is nothing truthful about him. He tells lies because he is by nature a liar. In fact, he is the father of all lies.

"For this reason, when I speak the truth, you do not believe me. Can anyone of you prove me guilty of sin? If not, then I must be speaking the truth. So why don't you believe me? The children of God listen to the words of their Father. Since you don't listen, you must not be his children." *(John 8:37–47)*

"BEFORE ABRAHAM WAS, I AM"

The Jewish people crowding around snapped back, "We've been right all along. You're not one of us. You're a Samaritan, and what's more, you're demon possessed."

"I am not demon possessed," I answered. "By my words and actions I honor my Father, but you dishonor me. I am not seeking praise for myself. There is one who wants me to receive praise, and he is also the one who judges. I tell you the truth, if a person obeys my teaching, he will never die."

At this the people exclaimed, "Now we know you've got a demon. You say that if a person obeys your teaching he will never die, yet Abraham and the prophets died. Apparently you think that you are greater than Abraham because he died. So also did the prophets. Who do you think you are?"

I replied, "If I honor myself, that honor is self-serving and worthless. My Father is the one who honors me. You say that he is your God although you do not know him at all. I am the one who knows him. If I said that were not true, I would be a liar just like you. But I know him, and I do what he says. Unlike you, your father Abraham rejoiced that he would see my day. He saw it and was glad."

Skeptically the people asked, "How could you have seen Abraham? You're not even fifty years old!"

"I tell you the truth," I responded, "before there was an Abraham, I AM." At this they started picking up stones to kill me, but I slipped away into the crowd and left the temple area. (John 8:48–59)

THE MAN BORN BLIND IS HEALED

As we were walking along, we met a man who was blind from birth. "Rabbi," asked the disciples, "was this man born blind because of his sins or the sins of his parents?"

I said to them, "His blindness has nothing to do with his sins or those of his parents. He was born blind so that we might see God at work in him. As long as it is day, we must do the works of him who sent me. Night is at hand when no one can work. So long as I am here in the world, I am the light of the world."

Then I spat on the ground and made some mud with the saliva. I daubed it on the eyes of the blind man and said, "Now go and wash your face in the pool of Siloam (the word means 'sent')." So the blind man went away and washed in Siloam. When he returned, he could see.

The man's neighbors who had seen him sitting and begging wondered whether this could be the same man. Some said, "Yes, he's the one."

Others said, "No, but he looks like the beggar."

But he himself kept telling them, "Look, I am that man!"

"But how is it possible that now you can see?" they asked.

The blind man answered, "A man named Jesus made some mud, daubed it on my eyes, and said, 'Go to Siloam and wash your face.' When I went there and washed, suddenly I was able to see."

"Where is that man?" they demanded.

"I don't know," the blind man answered.

The day on which I made mud and cured the blind man was a Sabbath. So the people brought the man to the Pharisees, who asked him how he had been cured of his blindness. He answered, "A man named Jesus put mud on my eyes. He told me to go and wash in Siloam; and when I did, I was able to see."

Some of the Pharisees said, "This man Jesus can't be from God, or he wouldn't have broken the Sabbath."

But others said, "How could a man who is a sinner perform such a miracle?"

They turned to the blind man and asked, "What do you say about him? After all, it was your eyes that he opened?"

"I think he's a prophet," answered the man.

But the Jewish authorities still did not believe that the man had once been blind. So they sent for his parents and asked, "Is this your son? Are you sure that he was born blind, and if so, how is it that now he can see?"

"Of course he's our son," the parents answered, "and obviously we know that he was born blind. But why he now can see, or who it was that restored his sight, we don't know. Why don't you ask him? After all, he is of age and able to speak for himself."

The man's parents answered in this way because they were afraid of the religious authorities. It had already been decided that anyone who held me to be the Messiah would be put out of the synagogue. That's why his parents said, "He is of age, ask him."

So once again the Pharisees summoned the man who had been born blind. "Own up and tell the truth," they said. "This man Jesus is a sinner!"

The man replied, "I don't know whether he is a sinner or not. But I do know that once I was blind but now I can see."

"What did he do to you?" they asked. "How did he cure your blindness?"

The man said, "I told you once and you paid no attention. Why do you want to hear it again? Could it be that you want to become his disciples?"

"No!" they shouted back in anger. "You are his disciple; we are disciples of Moses! We know that God gave the law to Moses. But as for this Jesus, we haven't the faintest idea where he came from."

"This is truly amazing," said the man. "I was blind, and he restored my sight, yet you don't know where he came from. Everybody knows that God doesn't hear the prayers of sinners but only the prayers of those who respect and obey him. Never in the history of the world have we heard of anyone able to heal the eyes of a person blind from birth. Jesus could do nothing if he weren't from God."

The Pharisees, hot with anger, blurted out, "You have been steeped in sin from birth. How dare you lecture us!" So they drove him out.

When I heard what they had done, I found the man and asked, "Do you believe in the Son of Man?"

"Who is he, sir?" the man replied. "Let me know so I can believe in him."

"You have already met him," I said. "What's more, he is the one talking with you right now."

The man said, "Lord, I believe," and bowed in reverence before me.

Then I told him, "By coming into the world I have brought judgment. As a result, those who are blind will see, but those who see will become blind."

When some of those standing by heard this, they asked, "Surely you're not implying that we Pharisees are blind?"

I answered, "If you were blind, you would not be guilty, but as it is, you claim to see, so your guilt continues." *(John 9:1–41)*

"I Am the Good Shepherd"

I said, "I tell you the truth, anyone who does not enter the sheepfold through the gate but sneaks in some other way is a thief and a robber. The true shepherd enters through the gate. The gate-keeper opens the gate for him, and the sheep recognize his voice. He calls them by name, and they follow him out.

"When all his sheep are out of the fold, the shepherd walks ahead of them on the way to pasture. The sheep follow him because they know his voice. They will not follow a stranger but will run away because they do not recognize his voice."

I told the people this parable, but they did not understand what it meant. So I explained it as follows:

"I am the gate for the sheep. All who came before me were thieves and robbers, but the sheep did not listen to them. I am the gate. All who enter the sheepfold through me will be saved. They will come in and go out and find pasture. Safety and nourishment will be theirs.

"The thief comes only to steal, kill, and destroy the flock. I have come that you may have life in all its fullness. I am the good shepherd. The good shepherd lays down his life for the sheep. The hireling is not like the shepherd, who owns the sheep. When the hireling sees a wolf coming, he runs for his life, leaving the sheep at risk. So the wolf attacks and scatters the flock. The hireling works for wages; he doesn't really care about the sheep.

"I am the good shepherd. I know my own sheep, and my sheep know me, just as the Father knows me and I know the Father; and I lay down my life for the sheep. I have other sheep that do not belong to this fold. They too will recognize my voice, and I will bring them in. There is to be but one flock with one shepherd.

"The Father loves me for laying down my life so that I may take it back again. No one takes my life from me. I lay it down of my own free will. The authority to lay it down and to take it back is mine. This is what my Father has ordered me to do." *(John 10:1–18)*

DIVISION AMONG THE JEWS AGAIN

Once again my words caused a sharp division among the people. Many said, "He is demon possessed, raving mad. Don't listen to a man like that!"

But others said, "How could anyone possessed by a demon say what he has been saying? Surely demons can't open the eyes of a blind man?" *(John 10:19–21)*

Chapter Twenty

MINISTRY IN JUDEA

ON DIVORCE AND CELIBACY

One day the Pharisees came intending to trap me with a trick question. "Is it lawful," they asked, "for a man to divorce his wife for no particular reason?"

I answered their question with a question: "What does the law of Moses say about that?"

They replied, "Moses said that a man could write a certificate of separation and send her on her way."

"You are right," I agreed, "but Moses made that provision because the people had become hard of heart. It wasn't intended that way in the beginning. I'm sure you've read in Scripture that from the beginning God made the race male and female. That's why a man leaves his father and mother and is united with his wife; the two become one flesh. Since it was God who made one out of two, let not any one separate them again."

When the disciples had gone into the house, I explained to them once again that if a man divorces his wife for any reason other than an illicit affair on her part, and then marries another woman, he is committing adultery. Furthermore, if she should desert her husband [the wife could not initiate a divorce] and marry another man, she too would be committing adultery.

The disciples reasoned, "If the divorce laws are so strict, perhaps it would be better never to marry in the first place."

I answered, "That may be acceptable for some, but not every man can live as a eunuch. There are eunuchs who were born that way and others who have become eunuchs for the kingdom of God. Some have that gift, so let it be." *(Matt. 19:3–12; Mark 10:2–12)*

I BLESS THE CHILDREN

One day some people came to me bringing little children, even infants. They wanted me to lay my hands on them and pray for them. The disciples began to chide those who brought the children, and when I became aware of it, I was indignant. Gathering the children, I said to the disciples, "Let the children come to me. Don't try to stop them! For the kingdom of heaven is made up of people like these little ones. Truly I say to you, whoever will not receive the kingdom of God like a little child will never get into it at all." Then I took the children into my arms, laid hands on them, and blessed them. Only then did I leave the area. *(Matt. 19:13–15; Mark 10:13–16; Luke 18:15–17)*

THE RICH YOUNG MAN

As I started out again for Jerusalem, a Jewish leader came running up, knelt before me, and asked, "Good Teacher, what good deed must I still do to be sure of life in the age to come?"

"Why do you call me good?" I asked, "and why are you questioning me about some special good deed you must do to enter the kingdom? There is only one who is perfectly good. But to answer your question, if you want to qualify for the coming kingdom, keep the commandments."

"Which ones?" asked the man.

I said, "Do not murder, do not commit adultery, do not steal, do not perjure yourself, do not cheat another person. Respect your father and mother, and love your neighbor as much as yourself."

"Master," replied the young man, "ever since I was a child, I have carefully obeyed all these commandments; what remains for me to do?"

I looked directly at him and with love said, "Only one thing remains for you to do; sell everything you have and give the money to the poor, and you will have treasure in heaven. Then come back and follow me."

When the young man heard this, his face fell, and he went away sad at heart because so great were his possessions. *(Matt. 19:16–22; Mark 10:17–22; Luke 18:18–23)*

ON RICHES AND THE REWARDS OF DISCIPLESHIP

Then I looked around at those who had heard this exchange and said, "Truly I say to you, how difficult it is for a rich person to enter the kingdom of God." (The disciples were startled at this because Jewish tradition held that wealth was a sign of God's approval.)

Once again I said, "Dear children, how difficult it is to enter the kingdom of God. It is easier for a camel to pass through the eye of a needle than for a rich person to enter the kingdom of God."

When the disciples heard this, they were dumbfounded. "Then who can ever be saved?" they asked.

Looking at them directly, I answered, "The salvation of a rich man [or a poor man for that matter] is impossible for man, but for God all things are possible."

Peter took the occasion to ask, "What about us? We've forsaken all to follow you. What's in store for us?"

I answered, "You can be sure that when the world is reborn and I have taken my seat on the throne of glory, you who have followed me will also sit on twelve thrones directing the affairs of the twelve tribes of Israel. You are the men who have stood by me in my trials; and now, as my Father has granted me kingdom authority, so do I confer on you that same authority. You will eat and drink at my table in the kingdom. And everyone who has left houses or brothers or sisters or father or mother or children or fields for my sake, the sake of the gospel, or the sake of God's kingdom will receive now in this age a hundred times as much—homes, brothers, sisters, mothers, children, and fields, along with persecution—and in the age to come, eternal life. But many who are first will be last, and the last will be first." *(Matt. 19:23–30; Mark 10:23–31; Luke 18:24–30)*

THE PARABLE OF THE LABORERS IN THE VINEYARD

"The kingdom of heaven is like a landowner who went out at daybreak to hire some men to work in his vineyard. He agreed to pay them the usual day's wage and sent them off to his vineyard. Mid-morning he went out again and saw some other men standing idle in the marketplace, so he said to them, 'Go and work in my vineyard, and I will pay you a fair wage.' So off they went. Then at noon, and again in the middle of the afternoon, he did the same thing. About an hour before the close of the workday, he went out once again and found yet another group. 'Why have you been here all day long with nothing to do?' he asked.

"They answered, 'Because no one has hired us.'

"So the landowner said, 'Well then, go and join the others at work in my vineyard.'

"That evening the owner told his foreman, 'Call in the men at work in the field and pay them their wages, beginning with those hired most recently and moving back to those hired first.'

"The men who had worked only one hour each received a full day's wage. So when those who had worked all day long came, they expected to receive more, but they too were paid a single day's wage. They took it but complained to their employer, 'Those other fellows worked only one hour, but you paid them the same as you paid us who did a full day's work in the hot sun.'

"The owner said to one of them, 'My friend, I have not treated you unfairly. Didn't you agree to work for the standard daily wage? Take what you have earned and go home. It was my decision to pay the latecomers the same as I paid you. Don't I have the right to do what I want with what belongs to me? Are you envious because I have been generous?' So those who are last will be first, and the first will be last.'" *(Matt. 20:1–16)*

THE FEAST OF DEDICATION IN JERUSALEM

It was winter when I arrived in Jerusalem for the festival of Dedication. I was walking in the section of the temple area known as Solomon's Porch when the Jewish leaders cornered me and asked, "How much longer do you intend to provoke us this way? If you are the Messiah, tell us so straight out."

I answered, "I did tell you, and you refused to believe me. The works that I do by my Father's authority make plain who I am. But you do not believe in me because you are not part of my flock. My sheep recognize my voice. I know them and they follow me. I give them eternal life, and they will never perish, for no one can snatch them out of my grip. My Father, who gave them to me, is more powerful than all, so they are absolutely safe in his hands. And I and the Father are one."

The Jewish leaders picked up stones intending to kill me, but I said to them, "You have seen me do many gracious and good deeds, made possible by the Father. For which one of them are you about to stone me?"

They answered, "It is not for some gracious and good deed that we are about to stone you. It is because you, a mere man, are claiming to be God. That is blasphemy and for that you must die!"

I answered, "In your Scripture does not God say, 'You are gods?' We know that Scripture cannot be in error, so if God called those people 'gods,' why do you say that I am guilty of blaspheming for saying, 'I am the Son of God?' After all, God set me apart for this role and sent me into the world. If I am not doing what my Father does, then you should not believe me. But if I am, you should believe me for that, even though you do not believe me for who I claim to be. Then you will come to know for certain that the Father is one with me. And I and the Father are one."

Once again they tried to arrest me, but I escaped out of their grasp. *(John 10:22–39)*

I WITHDRAW ACROSS THE JORDAN

After that encounter I crossed the Jordan River to the place where John used to baptize. There I remained for a while. Many people came to me saying that, although John had no miracle to validate his message, everything he said about me was true! A considerable number of those people came to believe in me. *(John 10:40–42)*

THE RAISING OF LAZARUS

A man named Lazarus lay sick in the village of Bethany. His two sisters, Mary and Martha, lived with him. (This was the same Mary who anointed me with expensive perfume and wiped my feet with her hair. It was her brother Lazarus who was sick). So the sisters sent me word, "Lord, your good friend is ill."

When I heard this, I said, "This illness won't end in death. Its purpose is to bring glory to God and so that I may be glorified through it."

I loved Martha, her sister Mary, and Lazarus. So after hearing that he was ill, I stayed where I was for two more days. Then I said to my disciples, "Let's go back to Judea."

"But Rabbi," they protested, "just a short time ago the people in Judea were trying to stone you! Why would you go there now?"

I answered, "There are twelve hours of daylight in every day. If you walk during the day, you have the light of the sun to keep you from stumbling. But if you walk at night, you will stumble because the sun has gone down." Then I added, "Our friend Lazarus has fallen asleep, and I am going to Bethany to wake him up."

The disciples were confused. "But Lord," they said, "if he has simply fallen asleep, he will be all right." They thought I was talking about normal sleep, but I meant that Lazarus had in fact died.

So I told them plainly, "Lazarus is dead! And for your sake I am glad that I was not there with him. This way your faith will have a chance to grow. Come, let's go to him."

Thomas (the disciple called "the Twin") said to the others, "We might as well go with him so we can die with him."

When we arrived in Bethany, I was told that Lazarus had already been in the tomb for four days. Bethany was less than two miles east of Jerusalem, so many of Mary and Martha's friends had come from the city to comfort the sisters over the loss of their brother.

When Martha got word that I had arrived, she hurried out to meet me. Mary, however, remained in the house. Martha exclaimed to me, "Lord, if you'd been here, my brother would not have died. But I know that even now God will do for you whatever you ask."

"Your brother Lazarus will live again," I said to Martha.

She answered, "I know that he will be raised to life on the last day, when all the dead are raised."

"I am the resurrection and the life," I declared. "All who believe in me will live, even though they die. And whoever lives and believes in me will never die. Do you believe this?"

"Yes, Lord," she replied. "I am convinced that you are the Messiah, the Son of God. You are the one who was to come into the world."

After saying this, Martha went back to Mary and quietly told her, "The Teacher is here and wants to see you." When Mary heard this, she got up quickly and came out to me. I was still outside the village, in the place where I had talked with Martha. The people from Jerusalem who had come to comfort Mary were still in the house. But when they saw her get up and go out, they followed her, thinking she was going to the tomb to weep.

Mary hurried out to be with me. When she saw me, she fell at my feet and cried, "Lord, if you'd been here, my brother would not have died!"

When I saw that Mary and her friends were weeping, I was deeply moved in spirit and visibly distressed. "Where have you laid him?" I asked.

"Come and see, Lord," they answered.

I burst into tears. The Jewish people who had come to mourn said, "See how much he loved Lazarus!"

Some of them said, "This man cured the eyes of the blind man. Why couldn't he have done something to keep Lazarus from dying?"

Deeply moved in spirit, I went to the tomb, which was a cave with a stone across the entrance.

"Roll away the stone," I ordered.

"But Lord," objected Martha, "by now the body will smell. It's been in the tomb for four days."

I said, "Didn't I tell you that if you believed, you would see the glory of God?"

So they rolled away the stone. Then I looked up to heaven and said, "Thank you, Father, for hearing my prayer. I know that you always answer my prayers, but I said this so all these people would believe that you sent me."

When I had finished my prayer, I called out in a loud voice, "Lazarus, Come out of there!" Suddenly the man who had died came out of the tomb, wrapped hand and foot with grave cloths and a towel around his face.

I said, "Unbind him, and let him go." *(John 11:1–44)*

THE CHIEF PRIESTS AND PHARISEES TAKE COUNSEL AGAINST ME

Many who had followed Mary from the house and seen the miracle that I had performed believed in me. But others went to the Pharisees to report what I had done. So the chief priests and the Pharisees called the council into session. "We haven't made much headway so far, have we?" they said. "This man is still performing miracles. If we let him get away with this, everyone will begin to believe in him. Then the Romans will get involved, and that could affect our prestige, to say nothing of putting our nation in jeopardy."

The high priest that year was a man by the name of Caiaphas. At this point he spoke up, saying, "You gentlemen have failed to think this matter through. Don't you realize that it would be better to have one man die for the people than for the entire nation to be destroyed?" Caiaphas didn't say this on his own, but as high priest that year, he was prophesying that I was about to die for the Jewish nation. And not for that nation only but also for the children of God scattered abroad, to bring them together and make them one. So from that day on, the council started planning how to put me to death. *(John 11:45–53)*

TROUBLE AHEAD IN JERUSALEM

As a result, I no longer went about openly in Jerusalem. Instead, I went to the desert town of Ephraim where I stayed with the disciples.

It was almost time for the Jewish festival of Passover. Many people from the rural areas throughout the country had gone up to Jerusalem to purify themselves in preparation for the Passover. They were on the lookout for me. Standing around in the temple area, they said to one another, "What do you think? You suppose he's decided not to come to the festival?"

The chief priests and Pharisees had issued an order that if anyone saw me they should report it immediately. That way I could be taken into custody. *(John 11:54–57)*

THE THIRD PREDICTION OF THE PASSION

As we continued toward Jerusalem, I walked on ahead of the disciples who were perplexed by my solemn demeanor. Both they and the crowd that followed sensed my determination and were apprehensive about the future. I motioned the Twelve to join me in private and began to tell them once again what was going to happen to me. "We are now on our way to Jerusalem," I said, "where everything the prophets foretold about me, the Son of Man, will come true. I will be handed over to the chief priests and the legal experts. They will condemn me to death and turn me over to the Romans who will treat me shamefully. They will mock me and spit on me. Then, after a severe flogging, they will put me to death; but three days later I will rise to life." The disciples, however, were unable to grasp the meaning of any of this because it was hidden from them; they did not understand what I was saying. *(Matt. 20:17–19; Mark 10:32–34; Luke 18:31–34)*

THE SONS OF ZEBEDEE: PRECEDENCE AMONG THE DISCIPLES

The wife of Zebedee came to me with her two sons, James and John. She knelt before me to ask for a special favor. "What do you want?" I asked.

She answered, "Promise me that when your kingdom comes, my two sons will be seated, one on your right side and one on your left."

"You don't realize what you are asking. Are you, James and John, able to drink the cup of suffering that I am about to drink or to be baptized with the baptism that I must endure?"

"Yes, we can!" they exclaimed.

I responded, "Yes indeed, you will drink a cup like mine and be baptized with a baptism like mine, but as for the seats on my right and on my left, they are not mine to assign. God has prepared them for the ones he has chosen."

When the other disciples heard what James and John had asked for, they became highly indignant. So I called them all together and said, "You are aware that in this world those who are considered rulers lord it over their subjects, and those in authority vaunt their power over others. But among you that is not the case. Whoever would be your leader must become your servant, and the one who would be first among you must serve everyone else. Even the Son of Man came to serve, not to be served, and to give up his life as a ransom for many." *(Matt. 20:20–28; Mark 10:35–45)*

THE HEALING OF BARTIMAEUS

As the disciples and I were leaving the old city of Jericho, a good-sized crowd followed along. Just outside the city sat a blind man by the name of Bartimaeus, begging from those on their way to Jerusalem. When he heard a crowd of travelers passing by, he asked what it was all about and was told that it was Jesus of Nazareth. At this he called out to me at the top of his voice, "Jesus, Son of David, take pity on me!" Many in the crowd around him insisted that he be quiet, but he shouted out all the louder, "Lord, Son of David, take pity on me!"

So I stopped and asked that someone would bring him to me. They relayed the message to the blind man, saying, "All is well; get up, he is calling for you." Throwing aside his coat, the man jumped up and came to me.

"What would you like me to do for you?" I asked.

"Master," he said, "I want to see again."

"You can go now," I responded. "Your faith has given you sight."

All at once he could see again. He began to follow us along the way, praising God; and the entire crowd joined in praise to

God for what they had seen with their own eyes. *(Matt. 20:29–34; Mark 10:46–52; Luke 18:35–43)*

ZACCHAEUS

Shortly after that, I arrived at the rebuilt Herodian town of Jericho. That was where an important and rich tax collector by the name of Zacchaeus lived. He was a short man, which made it difficult for him to see me in the crowd, although he kept trying. Judging that I was taking a certain route through town, Zacchaeus ran on ahead and climbed up into a sycamore tree so he could see me. When I reached that spot, I stopped and looked up at Zacchaeus. "Zacchaeus," I said, "come down from that tree right now, for I am going to be a guest at your house today."

So Zacchaeus climbed down as fast as he could and took me home with him, rejoicing all the way.

The crowd saw what had happened and began to complain, "This Jesus has gone to the home of a notorious sinner."

Zacchaeus objected to this put-down and said to me, "Here and now, Lord, I promise to give half my possessions to the poor, and if I have defrauded any one of anything, I will pay him back four times as much!"

And I said, "Today salvation has come to this man's household because he has shown himself to be a true son of Abraham. For the Son of Man has come to search for the lost and save them." *(Luke 19:1–10)*

THE PARABLE OF THE POUNDS

As we traveled along, the crowd was listening to everything I had to say. They were of the opinion that the kingdom of God was about to begin. When we arrived just outside Jerusalem, I told them this parable:

"A nobleman planned to go a distant country where he would be appointed king and then return. So he selected ten servants and gave each one a gold coin. Then he said to each, 'See how much you can earn with it while I am gone.'

"The nobleman's fellow citizens disliked him so intensely that they sent a delegation to the other country informing them that they didn't want this man to come back as king. However, the man was made king and returned to his own country. He summoned the servants to whom he had given money so he could find out how much each one had earned with the coin he had been given.

"The first servant said, 'Sir, I invested the gold coin you gave me and earned ten more.'

"'Well done,' said the king; 'you are a good servant. Because you have proven trustworthy in a small matter, I will now put you in charge of ten cities.'

"Then the second servant reported that he had earned five gold coins with the one he had received. And the king put him in charge of five cities.

"Then the other servant stepped forward and said, 'Sir, here is the gold coin you gave me. I wrapped it carefully in a piece of cloth and hid it where no one could find it. I was afraid of you because you are such a severe man, withdrawing money you didn't deposit and harvesting grain you didn't plant.'

"'You wicked servant!' snarled the king; 'your own words will condemn you. If you knew I was a severe man, withdrawing what I had not deposited and harvesting what I had not planted, why didn't you simply put the coin in the bank so when I returned I could draw it out plus interest?' Then to the others standing by, the king said, 'Take his coin and give it to the servant who has ten.'

"'But sir,' they exclaimed, 'that man already has ten!'

"'Correct,' said the king, 'those who use well what they are given will receive even more; but those who fail to use what they are given, what little they have will be taken away. As for the citizens who didn't want me to become king, round them up and execute them right here where I can watch.'" *(Luke 19:11–27)*

THE PLOT AGAINST LAZARUS

A number of people in Jerusalem learned that I was in Bethany. So they went there not only because I was there but also to see Lazarus whom I had raised from the dead. Because of Lazarus, many were abandoning the Jewish faith and beginning to believe in me. As a result, the chief priests were making plans to kill Lazarus as well. *(John 12:9–11)*

Chapter Twenty-One

FINAL MINISTRY IN JERUSALEM

THE TRIUMPHAL ENTRY

Although the chief priests were laying plans against both me, and Lazarus, I continued toward Jerusalem, walking on ahead of the others. As we approached the villages of Bethphage and Bethany, at the Mount of Olives, I sent two of my disciples ahead with these instructions: "Go into the village ahead of us, and just as you enter, you will see a donkey and by her side a colt that has never been ridden. Untie them and bring them to me. If anyone asks why you are taking the donkey and her colt, simply say, 'The Master needs them, but he will send them back as soon as he is done.' This will fulfill what the prophets, Isaiah and Zechariah, said: 'Tell the people of Israel, "Behold, your King is coming, humble and mounted on a donkey, on a colt, the foal of a beast of burden."'"

So the two disciples went on ahead and entered the village. There they found everything exactly as I had described it. The colt was tethered outside in the street. When the disciples started to untie it, the owners asked, "What are you doing, untying that colt?"

"The Lord has need of them," responded the disciples. So the owners let them bring the donkey and its colt back to me. Then the disciples threw their cloaks over the back of the colt and helped me mount. As Scripture says, "Fear not, people of Israel! Here comes your king, riding on a young donkey!"

Jerusalem was crowded with people who had come to celebrate Passover, and when they heard that I was on my way to the city, they took palm branches and rushed out to greet me. As I rode along, some spread their cloaks on the ground ahead of me, while others spread the greenery they had brought from the fields. They kept shouting, "Praise God! God bless the one who comes in the name of the Lord! God bless the long-awaited Messiah!"

When we reached the point where the road descends from the Mount of Olives to Jerusalem, the entire crowd burst out in joyful thanks to God, praising him at the top of their voices for all the wonderful miracles they had seen. Both those who went ahead and those who followed kept crying out, "Hosanna! Blessed is the one who comes in the name of the Lord! Blessed is the coming reign of King David, our father! Peace in heaven and glory to God in the highest heaven!"

At that time the disciples did not grasp the significance of what was taking place. However, after I was exalted, they came to understand that these events were in fulfillment of prophetic Scripture.

Those who were with me when I called Lazarus out of the tomb were telling everyone how I had brought a dead man back to life. A great number of people came to meet me because they heard that I had performed this miraculous sign.

Some Pharisees in the crowd called out, "Teacher, tell your followers to be quiet!"

I answered, "I tell you, if these followers of mine were to fall silent, the stones in the road would break out in jubilation."

Exasperated, the Pharisees said to one another, "You see, this is getting us nowhere. The whole world has gone after him." *(Matt. 21:1–9; Mark 11:1–10; Luke 19:28–40; John 12:12–19)*

I Weep over Jerusalem

When I drew near Jerusalem and saw the city spread out before me, I broke into tears. "If you had only recognized at this time what makes for peace! But now it is too late, and the way is hidden from your eyes. A time is coming when your enemies will throw up a barricade against you; they will encircle you and attack from every direction. They will destroy you completely, you and everyone within your walls. Not a single stone will be left in place because you were unaware that God had chosen this point in time to bring salvation." *(Luke 19:41–44)*

Reception by the Crowds

When I went into Jerusalem, the entire city was filled with excitement. "Who is this man?" everyone was asking.

The crowd of pilgrims answered, "He is the prophet Jesus who comes from Nazareth in Galilee."

When I entered the temple courts, the blind and the lame came to me, and I healed them. But when the chief priests and the legal experts saw the amazing things I was doing and heard the children in the temple courts shouting, "Hosanna to the Son of David," they were indignant and asked, "Do you hear what these children are saying?"

"Yes I do," I said, "but have you never read where Scripture says, 'You have ordained that the mouths of children and toddlers should break forth in praise.'" Then, leaving the temple, I went back to the town of Bethany where I spent the night. *(Matt. 21:10–11, 14–17; Mark 11:11; Luke 19:45–46)*

THE CURSING OF THE FIG TREE

The next morning, as I was returning to Jerusalem from Bethany, I was hungry. Some distance off I saw a fig tree in full leaf so I went to it in hopes of finding some fruit. Unfortunately I found nothing but leaves because it was still too early in the season for figs. So I said to the tree, "May no one ever eat your fruit again!" And my disciples heard me say this. *(Matt. 21:18–19; Mark 11:12–14)*

THE CLEANSING OF THE TEMPLE

When we arrived in Jerusalem, I went to the temple. There in the Court of the Gentiles, I saw merchants selling cattle, sheep, and doves for sacrifice. Others were sitting at their tables exchanging money. So I made a whip out of some pieces of cord and used it to drive them out of the temple, along with their sheep and cattle. I turned the tables of the money changers upside down, scattering their coins in every direction.

To those who were selling doves, I demanded, "Get them out of here! How dare you turn my Father's house into a marketplace!" I would not allow the courtyard to be used as a shortcut for those carrying temple vessels.

Then I began to teach them, saying, "Does not Scripture say, 'My house shall be called a house of prayer for people of every nation, but you are turning it into a hideout for thieves!'"

Then the disciples remembered what was prophesied in Scripture, "Zeal for my house will consume me." *(Matt. 21:12–13; Mark 11:15–17; Luke 19:45–46; John 2:13–17)*

THE CHIEF PRIESTS AND LEGAL EXPERTS CONSPIRE AGAINST ME

From then on I taught daily in the temple courts. The chief priests and legal experts, as well as the leading citizens, were looking for some way to destroy me but were unable because the people were captivated by what they were hearing. *(Mark 11:18–19; Luke 19:47–48)*

THE FIG TREE IS WITHERED

The next morning the disciples were walking by the place where I had cursed the fig tree. They noticed that it had dried up right down to the root. Peter exclaimed in surprise, "Master, look! The fig tree you cursed has withered and died! How did that happen so quickly?"

I answered, "I assure you that if you have faith and do not doubt, you will be able to do not only what I have done to this fig tree, but should you say to the mountain over there, 'May someone pick you up and throw you into the sea,' it will happen. That is why I tell you: Whatever you ask in prayer, believe that you have received it, and it will be yours. And when you stand up to pray, forgive anyone against whom you are holding a grudge, so that your Father in heaven may forgive the wrongs you have done." *(Matt. 21:20–22; Mark 11:20–26)*

THE QUESTION ABOUT AUTHORITY

When we arrived at Jerusalem and entered the temple courts, I was met by Jewish authorities who demanded that I show them some miraculous sign to prove that I had the authority to do what I was doing.

"Tear down this temple," I said, "and in three days I will build it up again."

"What!" they exclaimed. "This temple has been under construction for forty-six years. What makes you think you could rebuild it in three days?"

Of course, the temple to which I was referring was my own body. Later, when I had risen from the dead, the disciples remembered I had said this and believed both the Scripture and the words that I had spoken.

Later that week when I was teaching in the temple courts and preaching the good news, the leading priests, legal experts, and influential laypeople confronted me again. They demanded, "By what authority are you doing the things you do? Who gave you permission?"

I answered, "And I have a question for you. If you give me an answer to my question, I will tell you by what authority I do these things. 'Was the baptism of John from heaven or from men? Answer me that.'"

They began to reason among themselves, "If we say, 'From heaven,' he will want to know, 'Why then didn't you believe him?' But how can we say, 'From men,' since in that case the people—and frankly, we are afraid of them—will stone us because they are convinced that John was a genuine prophet." So they answered, "We don't know where his baptism came from."

I responded, "Since you won't answer my question, neither will I answer yours. I won't tell you the authority by which I do these things." *(Matt. 21:23–27; Mark 11:27–33; Luke 20:1–8; John 2:18–22)*

THE PARABLE OF THE TWO SONS

Then I told them this parable:

"There once was a man who had two sons. He went to the first and said, 'Son, go out and work in the vineyard today.'

"'No way,' said the son. However, a bit later he changed his mind and went out to work.

"In the meantime the father went to his second son and made the same request. This son responded, 'Of course, Father,' but he didn't go. So which of the two sons did what his father wanted?"

"The first," they all answered.

So I said to them, "I tell you the truth, tax collectors and prostitutes are going into the kingdom of God ahead of you. For John the Baptist appeared on the scene showing you how to live a righteous life, and you would not accept his teaching. But the tax collectors and prostitutes did. Even after you saw the change in their lives, you still did not repent and believe." *(Matt. 21:28–32)*

THE PARABLE OF THE WICKED TENANTS

"Once there was a landowner who planted a vineyard. He built a fence around it, dug a pit for stomping the grapes, and built a watchtower. Then he leased it out to vine growers and left on a long journey. When harvest time came, he sent several servants to the tenants to collect his share of the harvest. But the tenants seized the servants; one they beat and sent back empty-handed, one they killed, and one they stoned.

"So the landowner sent a larger group of servants to collect what was due him, and they were treated in the same way—some were flogged and others killed.

"Finally he sent his only son whom he dearly loved. He thought, 'Surely they will respect my son.' But when the tenants saw that he had sent his son, they said to one another, 'Look! Here comes the heir to the estate. Come on, let's kill him. Then we'll get everything that would have gone to him.'

"So they seized him, dragged him out of the vineyard and murdered him. Now when the owner of the vineyard returns, what do you think he will do to those tenants?"

The religious leaders answered, "He'll put those wretched scoundrels to a miserable death and lease the vineyard to tenants who will give him his rightful share each season when harvest comes around."

I asked, "Can it be that you have never read the text which says, 'The very stone which the builders rejected has become the cornerstone. This was done by the Lord and is marvelous to see.'

"For this reason the kingdom of God will be taken away from you and given to a people who live fruitful lives. Everyone who stumbles over that stone (the cornerstone) will be broken to pieces, and the one on whom it falls will be crushed."

The chief priests and Pharisees listened to these parables and began to realize that I was talking about them. They were the culprits. They wanted to take me into custody but were afraid of the crowds, who regarded me as a prophet. So they left me alone and went their way. *(Matt. 21:33–46; Mark 12:1–12; Luke 20:9–19)*

THE PARABLE OF THE MARRIAGE FEAST

Once more I taught them using a parable. I said:

"The kingdom of heaven is like a king who prepared a banquet for his son's wedding. He sent his servants to tell those who had been invited that the banquet was now ready, but they wouldn't come. So he sent other servants to them with the message: 'The wedding feast is ready! I've butchered the fattened livestock, and it's time for the banquet. Come! let's celebrate!'

"But the invited guests still paid no attention; one went out to his farm and another to his place of business. The others laid hold of the servants, mistreated them shamefully, and even killed some. The king was furious. He ordered his troops to kill those who had murdered his servants and to set their city ablaze.

"Then he said to his servants, 'The wedding feast is ready, but those I invited have proven unworthy, so go to the major crossroads of the city and invite to the wedding reception as many as you can find.' So the servants went and gathered all the people they could find, both bad and good, until the wedding hall was filled with guests.

"When the king came in to greet the guests, he noticed one who was not properly dressed for the occasion. 'My friend,' he said, 'how did you get in here without wedding clothes?' The man was speechless. Then the king said to his aides, 'Bind that man hand and foot and throw him outside in the dark. There he will weep and gnash his teeth.'" *(Matt. 22:1–14)*

On Paying Tribute to Caesar

Then the Pharisees met together to plan how they could trap me using my own words. They sent some of their disciples along with members of Herod's party to entrap me in my speech. This would give them grounds for turning me over to the authority and jurisdiction of the Roman governor. Feigning sincerity, they asked, "Teacher, we know that you are a man of integrity, truthful when you teach the way of God. You are not concerned with what others may think because social standing means nothing to you. So give us your opinion—is it proper to give poll tax to Caesar or not?"

Aware of their evil intentions, I replied, "You hypocrites! Why are you trying to trap me? Show me the coin required for the tax."

They brought me the Roman coin.

Then I said, "And whose image is this on the coin, and whose name?"

"Caesar's" they answered.

"Then give to Caesar what belongs to Caesar, and give to God what belongs to God."

Taken aback by my answer, they fell silent and slipped away. *(Matt. 22:15–22; Mark 12:13–17; Luke 20:20–26)*

THE QUESTION ABOUT THE RESURRECTION

That same day some Sadducees (who contend there is no resurrection) came to me with a question. "Teacher," they said, "Moses wrote that if a married man dies, leaving no children, his brother is to marry the widow so as to provide him with descendants. Now there was a family with seven sons. The oldest son married a woman but died without children, so the second son married the widow, but he too died childless. Then the third son married her, and so on through all seven sons. They all died without children. Finally, the woman herself died. Now here is the question: Whose wife will she be in the resurrection when all seven sons are raised? After all, each one had been her husband."

I replied, "Your question reveals that you don't understand the Scriptures or the power of God. In this age men and women marry, but in the age to come, following the resurrection, people will not marry. They will be like the angels in heaven and can never die. They are children of God, children of the resurrection.

"And in the passage about the burning bush, Moses clearly implied that the dead do rise. He refers to the Lord as 'the God of

Abraham, the God of Isaac, and the God of Jacob'—patriarchs who had died long before. God is not the God of the dead but of the living, for he has taken the righteous 'dead' into his realm of life."

"Teacher," exclaimed some legal experts, "that was a good answer." But they didn't have the courage to ask him anything else. *(Matt. 22:23–33; Mark 12:18–27; Luke 20:27–40)*

THE GREAT COMMANDMENT

Now when the Pharisees heard that I had silenced the Sadducees with my reply, they came to me as a group, and one of them, an expert in religious law, tried to trap me with this question: "Teacher," he said, "which commandment in the law is the most important?"

I answered, "The most important commandment is, 'Listen, O Israel! The Lord our God is the only Lord, and you shall love the Lord your God with all your heart, with all your soul, with all your mind, and with all your strength.' The second is equally important, 'You shall love the other person as you love yourself.' No other commandment is as important as these."

The expert in religious law exclaimed, "That was an excellent answer, Teacher. What you have said is true: God is one, and beside him there is no one else; and we are to love him with all our heart, with all our mind, and with all our strength, and to love the other person as we love ourselves. To fulfill these commandments is far more important than to offer up whole burnt offerings and sacrifices."

When I saw how sensibly he answered, I said to him, "You are not far from the kingdom of God."

From that point on no one had the courage to ask me any more questions. *(Matt. 23:34–40; Mark 12:28–34)*

THE QUESTION ABOUT DAVID'S SON

Some Pharisees gathered around me as I was teaching in the temple courts, so I asked them this question, "What do you think about the Christ? Whose son is he?"

"He is the Son of David," they responded.

"Then why, in the book of Psalms, does David call him Lord?" I asked. "David himself, under the inspiration of the Spirit, wrote: 'The Lord said to my Lord, Sit at my right hand until I have put your enemies under your feet.' If David calls Christ his Lord, how can Christ also be his son?"

No one was able to answer me, and from that day on no one dared to question me further. *(Matt. 22:41–46; Mark 12:35–37a; Luke 20:41–44)*

WOE TO THE SCRIBES AND PHARISEES

I continued to warn my disciples and the crowds against the religious leaders of Israel. I said:

"The legal experts and the Pharisees are the authorized teachers of the law of Moses. So you must faithfully carry out everything they tell you to do. However, don't imitate the way they live because they don't practice what they preach. They load the heavy burden of ritual obligation on the backs of their followers but refuse to lift a finger to help.

"Everything they do is designed to call attention to themselves. For example, they attach Bible verses to their foreheads and wear robes with extra long tassels. They love to be seated at the head table at banquets and given front row seats in the synagogue. It pleases them to be greeted with respect in the marketplace and have people address them as 'Rabbi.' But no one is to be regarded as 'the rabbi,' for you are all equal and have only one Teacher. Don't refer to anyone here on earth as 'Father' since you have but one Father, and he is in heaven. Nor are you to be called instructors since you have but one instructor, and I am that one. The one who ranks highest among you is the one who serves the other.

"How dreadful it will be for you legal experts and Pharisees! You hypocrites! You block the door to the kingdom of heaven so no one can get in. You don't go in yourself, and you get in the way of those trying to get in. You cheat widows out of their homes while pretending to pray for them. Your punishment will be severe.

"How dreadful it will be for you legal experts and Pharisees! You hypocrites! You will go anywhere in the world to make a single convert; and when you succeed, you make him twice as fit for hell as yourself.

"How dreadful it will be for you blind guides! You teach that if someone swears by the temple, the oath is not binding, but if he swears by the gold in the temple, that promise must be kept. You blind fools! Can't you see that the temple is more important than the gold that is in it? It's the temple that makes the gold sacred, not the other way around. You say, 'Whoever swears by the altar is not bound by his oath, but whoever swears by the gift he has placed on the altar is obliged to carry through.' How blind you are! Can't you see that the altar makes the gift sacred and is therefore of greater value? To swear by 'the altar' is to swear not only by the altar but by everything that's on it, and to swear 'by the temple' is to swear not only by the temple but by the One who dwells there. When you swear by heaven, you are swearing by the throne of God and the One sitting there.

"How dreadful it will be for you legal experts and Pharisees! You hypocrites! You are careful to give God a tenth part of your small garden herbs, such as mint, dill, and cumin; but you have neglected the weightier matters of the law, such as justice, mercy, and faithfulness. These things you ought to do without neglecting the others. You blind guides! You filter your wine so you won't accidentally swallow a ceremonially unclean gnat, yet you gulp down a camel.

"How dreadful it will be for you legal experts and Pharisees! You hypocrites! You scour the outside of a cup and dish but leave the inside full of what you have gained by violence and self-indulgence. You blind Pharisee! Clean the inside of the cup and dish first, and then the outside will be clean as well.

"How dreadful it will be for you legal experts and Pharisees! You hypocrites! You are like tombs freshly whitewashed. They appear beautiful on the outside, but inside they are full of dead men's bones and corruption of every sort. It's the same with you; on the outside you appear to be righteous, but inside you are full of hypocrisy and disobedience.

"How dreadful it will be for you legal experts and Pharisees! You hypocrites! You build tombs for the prophets and decorate the monuments of the righteous, saying, 'If we had lived in the days of our ancestors, we would never have joined them in shedding the blood of the prophets.' Thus you are testifying against yourselves because you are the descendants of those who murdered the prophets.

"Go on, then, finish off what your ancestors began! You serpents, you brood of snakes! How can you escape being sentenced to hell? This is why I continue to send you prophets, wise men, and legal experts—some of whom you will crucify, some you will kill, and others you will scourge in your synagogues having hunted them down in town after town. As a result you will be held responsible for the murder of all innocent people, from the murder of Abel the righteous to the murder of Zechariah the son of Barachiah,

whom you murdered between the sanctuary and the altar. I speak
the truth; the punishment for all these crimes will fall on you,
the people of this generation." *(Matt. 23:1-36; Mark 12:37b-40;
Luke 20:45-47)*

LAMENT OVER JERUSALEM

"Oh Jerusalem, Jerusalem! You who kill the prophets and stone
the messengers God sends to you. How often I have longed to gather
you in my arms as a hen gathers her chicks under her wings, but
you wouldn't let me. Look, there is your temple, forsaken by God!
For I tell you that you will never see me again until you say, 'Blessed
is the one who comes in the name of the Lord!'" *(Matt. 23:37-39;
Luke 13:34-35)*

THE WIDOW'S GIFT

One day in the temple, I sat down in the court of the women
to watch people as they dropped their money into the treasury
chest. Many rich people were putting in a great number of coins.
Then a poor widow came along and dropped in two little copper
coins, worth perhaps one penny. I called my disciples together and
said to them, "I tell you the truth, this poor widow has put more
into the treasury chest than all the others. For they gave what
they could easily spare, but she gave what she needed to live on."
(Mark 12:41-44; Luke 21:1-4)

Chapter Twenty-Two

MY TEACHING ABOUT THE LAST DAYS

I PREDICT THE DESTRUCTION OF THE TEMPLE

As we were leaving the temple, one of the disciples called our attention to the beauty of the buildings that made up the complex. "Master," he exclaimed, "look at the size and grandeur of those enormous stones. How magnificent is the temple and its courts!"

"You see those buildings?" I said. "Not a single stone will be left on top of another. They will all lie scattered on the ground." *(Matt. 24:1–2; Mark 13:1–2; Luke 21:5–6)*

SIGNS BEFORE THE END

We made our way up the Mount of Olives, sat down, and looked back at the temple. Several of the disciples—Peter, James, John, and Andrew to be specific—came to me privately, wanting to know when everything I had prophesied would come to pass. How could they know when I would return and the world would come to an end?

I warned my disciples about charlatans who would lead them astray. I said, "Many will come claiming to speak for me, saying, 'I am the Christ,' and, 'Time has run out, and the end is at hand.' Don't let them fool you. You will hear about wars and the threat of wars, but don't be alarmed. These things must happen, but the end is still to come. Nation will war against nation and kingdom against kingdom. There will be earthquakes and famines everywhere. Terrifying sights and signs will fill the heavens. All this is but the birth pangs of the new age." *(Matt. 24:3–8; Mark 13:3–8; Luke 21:7–11)*

PERSECUTION WILL COME

"When this terrifying time comes, keep a level head. Those in authority will hand you over to local councils who will flog you right there in their synagogues. They will drag you before governors and kings for no reason other than that you are known as a 'Christian.' This will be your opportunity to tell them about me. When you are put on trial, don't be anxious about what you are to say. Don't rehearse your defense beforehand because the Holy Spirit will tell you at that crucial time what you should say. Since he is the one who will be speaking through you, your adversaries will not be able to refute what you say.

"Brother will betray brother to death and a father his own child. Children will turn against parents and have them put to death. Yet none of you will be destroyed in an ultimate sense. You will be hated by everyone because you bear my name. At that time many will renounce their faith. Exchanging love for hate, they will sell their friends down the river. False prophets will appear, and many people will be led astray. Evil will become so rampant that men's love for one another, as well as for God, will grow cold. However, those who stand firm to the end will be saved. And the glad message of the kingdom will be proclaimed throughout the entire world so that every nation will hear. Only after that will the end come." *(Matt. 24:9–14; Mark 13:9–13; Luke 21:12–19)*

THE DESOLATING SACRILEGE

"When you see the Holy City surrounded by armies, then you will know that Jerusalem is about to be destroyed. And when you see what Daniel the prophet called 'the abomination of desolation' standing in the holy place, then it is time for action.

"Those of you who are in Judea must escape to the hills. If anyone is on the housetop, he should not waste time going down to pick up his belongings. Whoever is out in the field should not return to change clothing. Those are the days of divine vengeance when all the prophecies of Scripture will be fulfilled.

"How terrible it will be in those days for women who are pregnant and mothers who are nursing infants! Pray that you will not have to make your escape in winter or on a Sabbath day. For the suffering of that time will be greater than at any time since the world began or ever will be. Some will be killed by the sword, and others taken captive to nations around the world. Jerusalem will be trampled down by heathen until their time of domination is over." *(Matt. 24:15–22; Mark 13:14–20; Luke 21:20–24)*

FALSE MESSIAHS AND FALSE PROPHETS

"If someone says to you, 'Look! There is the Messiah!' or 'There he is over there!' don't believe him. For false messiahs and false prophets will appear and perform great miracles and wonders to deceive, if possible, even God's chosen people. Remember, I have warned you ahead of time.

"If someone says, 'The Messiah is out in the wilderness!' don't rush out to look for him; or if they say, 'He's hiding right here among us!' don't believe it. The coming of the Son of Man will be clear to all because my return will be like lightning flashing across the sky from east to west. When you see the vultures gather, you know they've found a corpse." *(Matt. 24:23–28; Mark 13:21–23)*

MY TRIUMPHAL RETURN FORETOLD

"Soon after the distress of those days, the sun will grow dark, and the moon will no longer give its light; the stars will fall from the sky, and the celestial powers will be shaken. On earth, nations will be in distress, bewildered by the roaring sea and surging waves. People will faint from fear as they wait for what is coming on the world. Then the sign of the Son of Man will appear in heaven, and all the tribes of the earth will beat their breasts in mourning. They will see me arriving on the clouds of heaven with overwhelming power and glory. The great trumpet will sound, and in triumph I will send out my angels to gather my people from the four winds, from one end of creation to the other." *(Matt. 24:29–31; Mark 13:24–27; Luke 21:25–28)*

THE PARABLE OF THE FIG TREE

"Listen to what the fig tree has to teach you. When its sprouts become tender and begin to thrust out leaves, you can see for yourself that summer is just around the corner. In the same way, when you see all these signs, know that the time is near, about to begin.

"I tell you the truth, all these things will begin to take place before the generation now alive has passed away. The time will come when heaven and earth will be no more, but what I say will remain forever. As for the specific day and hour of my return, no one knows, not even the angels in heaven, nor I. That knowledge belongs to the Father alone." *(Matt. 24:32–36; Mark 13:28–32; Luke 21:29–33)*

"TAKE HEED, WATCH!"

"Since you do not know exactly when the end will come, you must stay awake and be on your guard. Stay clear of a careless lifestyle of feasting and drinking coupled with the worries of this life, or that day will spring shut on you like a trap.

"The end will come suddenly and violently on all who live anywhere on the face of the earth. It will be like a man who put his servants in charge of various tasks, reminded the doorkeeper to stay alert, then left home for a long journey. So stay alert because you do not know when the owner of the house will return; it could be anytime—in the evening, around midnight, toward daybreak, or at sunrise. If the owner arrives without warning, he must not find you asleep. Pray that you will have the strength to endure all that is going to happen, and stand approved before the Son of Man.

"What I say to you I say to everyone: 'Watch for my return!'" *(Mark 13:33–37; Luke 21:34–36)*

Chapter Twenty-Three

FINAL MINISTRY PRIOR TO PASSION

THE NEED FOR WATCHFULNESS

"When the Son of man returns, it will be as it was in the time of Noah. In those days before the great flood people were eating and drinking, getting married, right up to the day that Noah went into the ark. They were oblivious to what was happening until the flood came and swept them away. That's the way it will be when I return. Two men will be working in the field; one will be taken and the other left. Two women will be together grinding grain; one will be taken and the other left. Watch, therefore, because you do not know what day I will come.

"You may be sure that if the owner of the house had known at what hour of the night the burglar would come, he would have stayed awake and prevented him from breaking in. You, too, must always be ready, for I will come when you least expect me." *(Matt. 24:37–44)*

THE PARABLE OF THE TEN VIRGINS

I told them the following parable to help them understand the kingdom of God:

"Once there were ten bridesmaids who took their torches and went out to meet the bridegroom. Five of them were foolish, and the other five were sensible. The foolish ones took their torches but no extra oil while the sensible ones took their torches plus flasks of oil. The bridegroom was late in coming so the girls became drowsy and fell asleep. Then at midnight came the shout, 'Here comes the bridegroom! Let's go out to meet him!'

"All ten bridesmaids woke up and were getting their torches ready. The foolish said to the wise, 'We need some of your oil because our torches are burning low.'

"'No,' the wise replied, 'there's not enough for all of us. You need to go to a shop and buy some oil for yourselves.'

"So the foolish bridesmaids hurried off to buy some oil, but before they could get back, the bridegroom had arrived. The sensible bridesmaids escorted him into the banquet room, and the door was closed. A bit later the foolish bridesmaids arrived and, standing outside, called out, 'Lord, Lord, open the door for us.'

"But he called out to them, 'Certainly not, I don't know who you are.'"

Applying the parable, I reminded my listeners to remain alert because they had no way of knowing either the day or the hour when I would return. *(Matt. 25:1–13)*

THE PARABLE OF SERVANTS—FAITHFUL AND WORTHLESS

This next parable explains what the kingdom of heaven will be like:

"There was a man of means, about to go abroad, who called his servants together and entrusted his wealth to them. To one he gave five thousand coins, to another two thousand, and to a third, one thousand—to each according to his ability. Then he left on the trip. The servant who received five thousand went out and invested it, netting 100 percent profit. The one who received two thousand also invested his money, gaining another two thousand. But the servant who received one thousand went out, dug a hole in the ground, and hid his master's money in it.

"Now after a long time, the master returned from abroad and settled accounts with his servants. The one who had received five thousand coins came in and handed him another five thousand. 'Sir,' he said, 'You entrusted me with five thousand coins. Look, here are five thousand more that they have earned.'

"'Well done, you good and faithful servant,' said the master. 'You have shown yourself trustworthy in handling a trivial matter, so I will let you exercise your ability in more important areas. Come and share your master's delight.'

"Next the servant who had received two thousand coins came and said, 'Sir, you entrusted me with two thousand coins. Look, here are an additional two thousand that they have earned.'

"'Well done, you good and faithful servant,' said the master. You have shown yourself trustworthy in handling a trivial matter, so I will let you exercise your ability in more important areas. Come and share your master's delight.'

"Then the servant who had received one thousand coins came and said, 'They told me that you were a hard man, harvesting where you hadn't sown and winnowing when you hadn't planted, so I was afraid. I took your coins and buried them in the ground. Look, here is your money; you now have what belongs to you.'

"But his master replied, 'You lazy and wicked servant! So you thought that I harvest where I haven't sown and winnow where

I haven't planted. Then why didn't you take the money and put it in the bank? At least, when I returned, I would have gotten my money back plus the interest.' Then the master ordered, 'Take the thousand coins from him and give them to the servant who has ten thousand. The one who has faithfully used what God has entrusted to him will see it grow and grow while the one who fails to use his gift will have it taken away. As for that worthless servant, throw him into the outer darkness, where men weep and gnash their teeth.'" (Matt. 25:14–30)

THE LAST JUDGMENT

"When the Son of Man comes in glory at the end of this age, accompanied by the angelic hosts, he will take his seat on the throne of glory. All the nations of the world will stand before me, and I will separate the people into two groups, just like a shepherd separates his sheep from his goats. I will put the sheep on my right and the goats on my left. Then I will say to those on my right, 'Come, you who are blessed by my Father, and inherit the kingdom reserved for you from the creation of the world. For I was hungry and you fed me, I was thirsty and you gave me something to drink, I was a stranger and you invited me in, I needed something to wear and you gave me clothes, I was sick and you took care of me, I was in prison and you came to my side.'

"Then the upright (the sheep) will ask, 'Lord, when did we see you hungry and fed you or thirsty and gave you something to drink? When did we ever see you a stranger and invite you in or needing something to wear and gave you clothes? And when was it that we saw that you were sick and took care of you or in prison and came to your side?'

"And I will answer, 'I tell you the truth, whenever you helped one of the least important of these followers of mine, you helped me.'

"Then to those on his left (the goats), I will say, 'Away from me, you that bear the curse of God! Away to the eternal fire prepared for the devil and his demons! For I was hungry and you gave me nothing to eat; I was thirsty and you offered me nothing to drink; I was a stranger and you showed me no hospitality, in need of clothing and you gave me nothing to wear, sick and in prison and you showed no concern for me.'

"Then they too will ask, 'Lord, when did we see you hungry or thirsty or a stranger or needing clothing or in prison and did not come to your help?'

"And I will answer, 'I tell you the truth, whenever you failed to help one of the least important of these, you failed to help me.' So these goats will be sent to the place of eternal punishment but the sheep to eternal life." *(Matt. 25:31–46)*

A SUMMARY OF MY FINAL DAYS IN JERUSALEM

I spent each day teaching in the temple courts, but when evening came, I would leave the city and spend the night on the Mount of Olives. Early each morning the people would flock to the temple courts to listen to me. *(Luke 21:37–38)*

SOME GREEKS SEEK ME OUT

Among those who had come to Jerusalem for Passover were some Greeks. They approached Philip (of Bethsaida in Galilee) and asked, "Sir, we would like to meet Jesus." Philip told Andrew, and the two of them came and told me.

I said, "The hour has now come for the Son of Man to be exalted. I tell you the truth, for a grain of wheat to become more than a single grain, it must fall into the ground and die. Only if it dies will it produce more grain. In the same way, if you hold on to your life you will lose it, but if you let it go in this world, you will keep it forever. If you want to serve me, you must live as I live. That way we will both be living in obedience to the will of God. If you serve me, my Father will honor you.

"Now is my heart deeply troubled. And what am I to say? 'Father, deliver me from this hour'? But for this very purpose I have come to this hour! Father, bring honor to your name!"

Then from heaven came a voice: "I have already brought honor to my name, and I will do it again."

When the crowd that was standing there heard the voice, some thought it was thunder. Others said, "No, it was an angel speaking to Jesus."

I told the crowd, "That voice was not for my benefit but for yours. The time for judging the people of this world has come. The prince of this world is about to be banished. When I am lifted up on the cross, I will draw everyone to myself. (I spoke of being "lifted up" so people would know what kind of death I would die)."

The crowd spoke up, "Our law says that the Messiah will live forever. How then can you say that the Son of Man must be 'lifted up'? Who is this Son of Man?"

I replied, "The light will be with you for only a little longer, so keep walking while you still have light. When darkness overtakes a traveler, he has no idea where he is going. Have faith in me while I am still with you, and you will become children of light." (John 12:20–36)

THE UNWILLINGNESS TO BELIEVE

When I had finished speaking, I withdrew from the center of attention. I had performed many miraculous signs in the presence of the people, but they still would not believe in me. Their unwillingness to believe fulfilled the prophecy of Isaiah, who said: "Lord, is there anyone who has believed our message? Has your miraculous power awakened faith in anyone?"

The people could not believe because elsewhere Isaiah said: "The Lord has blinded their eyes and hardened their hearts, so they cannot see with their eyes or understand with their minds. If they did, they would turn to the Lord and be healed." Isaiah said this because he saw the glory of Christ, and spoke of me.

Many of the Jewish leaders believed that I was the Christ, but because of the Pharisees, they would not confess it openly. They were afraid of being put out of the synagogue. They loved the adulation of people more than the praise that comes from God. *(John 12:37–43)*

JUDGMENT BY THE WORD

I raised my voice and spoke up so all could hear, "To believe in me is to believe not only in me but also in the one who sent me. And whoever sees me is seeing the one who sent me. I am the light that has come into the world so that those who believe in me should no longer have to walk in darkness.

"I am not the one who will pass judgment on those who hear my words but refuse to accept them. My purpose in coming is to save people, not to condemn them. But those who reject me and refuse to accept my teachings do have a judge. On the last day they will be judged by the words I have spoken. I have not spoken on my own authority. I have said only what the Father who sent me has commanded me to say. And I know that his command leads to eternal life. That is why I tell you exactly what the Father has told me to say." *(John 12:44–50)*

THE CONSPIRACY AGAINST ME

When I finished teaching these truths, I turned to my disciples and said, "You know that in two days the Feast of Unleavened Bread (the Passover) will be here, and I will be handed over to be crucified."

Meanwhile, some leading priests and influential laypeople were meeting in the palace of Caiaphas, the high priest, scheming how to arrest me away from public view and put me to death. "Not during the feast," they agreed, "or the people may riot." *(Matt. 26:1–5; Mark 14:1–2; Luke 22:1–2)*

THE ANOINTING AT BETHANY

Several days before the Passover I was having dinner in a home in the town of Bethany. (At Bethany I had raised Lazarus from the dead.) A woman entered the room with an alabaster jar of expensive perfume. She broke the long neck of the flask and poured about a pint of oil on my head and feet. Then she wiped my feet with her hair. The entire house was filled with the fragrance of the perfume.

When the disciples saw what was happening, they became indignant. "Why was expensive perfume wasted like that?" they complained. Judas Iscariot (the disciple who later betrayed me), said, "That perfume was worth a year's wages! Why wasn't it sold and the money given to the poor?" He said this not because he cared about the poor but because he was a thief. He had been entrusted with the money bag and would often help himself to whatever he wanted.

I said to them, "Why are you criticizing this woman for such a beautiful expression of devotion? Leave her alone. As for the poor, you will always have them, but you won't always have me. Pouring the ointment on my body was her way of preparing me for burial. I tell you the truth, wherever in the world the message of my death and resurrection is proclaimed, what this woman has done will be told as a memorial to her." *(Matt. 26:6–13; Mark 14:3–9; John 12:1–8)*

JUDAS PLANS TO BETRAY ME

Then Satan entered the heart of Judas Iscariot, one of the Twelve. He went to the leading priests and officers of the temple guard to discuss with them a scheme he had in mind. He asked, "How much are you willing to give me if I deliver him into your hands?" They were delighted with the proposal and offered to pay him thirty pieces of silver. From that point on Judas kept watching for a chance to betray me when no crowd was present. *(Matt. 26:14–16; Mark 14:10–11; Luke 22:3–6)*

Chapter Twenty-Four

THE LAST SUPPER

PREPARATION FOR THE PASSOVER

It was the first day of the Feast of Unleavened Bread, the day on which the Passover lamb was sacrificed. Peter and John came to me asking, "Where do you want us to go and prepare your Passover meal?"

I told them to go into Jerusalem where they would be met by a man carrying a water jug. They were to follow him. In whatever house he entered, they were to say to the owner, "The Teacher says that his time has come and would like to observe the Passover at your house. Where is the guest room in which he and his disciples are to eat the Passover?' He will show you a large upstairs room, furnished with couches and ready. That's where you are to prepare the Passover meal." So the disciples left and went into the city where they found everything just as I had told them. They prepared the Passover meal, and when evening came, we shared the meal. *(Matt. 26:17–20; Mark 14:12–17; Luke 22:7–14)*

I Wash the Disciples' Feet

Passover was beginning, and I knew that the time had come for me to leave this world and return to my Father. Throughout my ministry I had always loved my own, and now I was about to show them the full extent of my love.

Even before the evening meal had gotten underway, the devil had convinced Judas Iscariot, Simon's son, that he should betray me.

I knew that God had placed everything under my control. I also knew that I had come from God and that I was soon to return to him. So I rose from the table and removed my robe. Taking a towel, I tied it around my waist. Pouring some water into a washbasin, I began to wash the disciples' feet, drying them with the towel around my waist.

But when I came to Simon Peter, he asked in astonishment, "Lord, could you possibly intend to wash my feet?"

I answered, "What I am doing right now you won't fully understand, but in time you will grasp what it means."

"You'll never wash my feet!," insisted Peter.

"If I do not wash you," I replied, "you will no longer be one of mine."

"In that case, Lord," exclaimed Peter, "don't stop at washing my feet; pour water all over me!"

I responded, "If a person has had a complete bath, there is no need to wash except for his feet. And you are clean—all except one." I knew who was about to betray me, and that is why I said that they were all clean "except one."

When I had finished washing their feet, I put on my robe and returned to my place at table. Then I asked, "Do you understand what I have just done to you? You call me your teacher and Lord, and you are right to do so because that is what I am. Since I, your teacher and Lord, have just washed your feet, you should do the same for one another. I have given you an example so that you will do for one another what I have done for you. I tell you the truth, a servant is not superior in rank to his master; a messenger is not greater than the one who sends him. Now that you know these things, you will be blessed by God if you do them.

"I am not talking about all of you; I know those I have chosen. But the Scripture must be fulfilled that says, 'The one who has shared my table has lashed out against me.'

"I am telling you this before it happens. That way, when it does, you will believe that I am the one I claim to be. I tell you the truth, whoever accepts one of my messengers, accepts me. And whoever accepts me, accepts the one who sent me." *(John 13:1–20)*

ONE OF THE TWELVE WILL BETRAY ME

While we were eating, I warned my disciples that one of them would betray me. I said, "I tell you the truth, one of you is going to double-cross me. That one is sharing this meal. The Son of Man must die, just as it is foretold in Scripture, but woe to the one who will betray me! It would have been better for him never to have been born in the first place." I was profoundly disturbed in spirit and said to them, "I tell you the truth, one of you is going to betray me."

The disciples were stunned! They looked around at each other at a loss to know which of them I meant. One after the other kept asking, "Surely, Lord, I'm not the one, am I?"

The disciple commonly known as "the one Jesus loved" was sitting next to me. Simon Peter motioned to him to find out to whom I was referring. So he leaned back against me and asked, "Lord, who is it?"

I replied, "I am going to dip this piece of bread in the sauce and give it to the one who will betray me."

Then Judas, the traitor, said, "Surely, Rabbi, I'm not the one, am I?"

I answered, "It is just as you have said."

Then I dipped the bread and gave it to Judas Iscariot, Simon's son. As soon as Judas took the bread, Satan took complete possession of him.

"Go ahead and do what you intend," I said.

No one at table understood what I meant by that. Since Judas was in charge of the money bag, some thought I had told him to buy whatever was needed for the festival. Others thought that perhaps he was to give some money to the poor. Judas took the piece of bread and left the room immediately.

It was night. *(Matt. 26:21–25; Mark 14:18–21; Luke 22:14, 21–23; John 13:21–30)*

OUR LAST SUPPER

I said to my disciples, "I wanted very much to eat this last Passover meal with you before I began my suffering, for I tell you, I will not eat it again until its full meaning is fulfilled in the kingdom of God."

While we were eating, I took some bread and, after giving thanks, I broke it in pieces and handed it to my disciples, saying, "Here, take this bread and eat it. It represents the giving of my body for you. Do it as a memorial to me." Then I took the wine cup and, when I had given thanks, said, "You must all drink from it, for it represents my blood, the blood of the new covenant, poured out as a sacrifice for the forgiveness of sins. Truly I say to you, I will never drink it again until that day in my Father's kingdom when we'll drink it anew." *(Matt. 26:26–29; Mark 14:22–25; Luke 22:15–20)*

THE LEADER AS SERVANT

An argument arose among the disciples as to which of them should be regarded as the greatest. So I said, "Pagan rulers lord it over their subjects and give themselves the title Friends of the People, but it must not be like that with you. Rather, the one in a position of authority among you must be one who performs menial tasks; the leader must take the servant's role. Who is thought to be more important, the one who sits at the table or the one who serves? Is it not the one who sits at table? Yes, but I am among you as one who serves.

"You have stood by me in my trials. So just as my Father has assigned me the power to rule, so I extend the same right to you. You will eat and drink at my table in my kingdom and sit on thrones ruling over the twelve tribes of Israel." *(Luke 22:24–30)*

THE NEW COMMANDMENT OF LOVE

After Judas left, I said, "Now, at last, I am about to enter into my glory, and this will bring glory to God. After God receives glory because of me, he will not delay in bringing glory to me.

"My children, I will be with you only a little longer. You will look for me, but as I told the Jewish authorities, 'You cannot go where I am going.' Now I give you a new commandment: Love one another. You are to love one another as I have loved you. Your love for one another will demonstrate to everyone that you truly are my disciples." *(John 13:31–35)*

Chapter Twenty-Five

THE FAREWELL DISCOURSE

"LET NOT YOUR HEARTS BE TROUBLED"

"Don't worry about my going away. I know you trust in God, so put your trust in me as well. There's plenty of room for everyone in my Father's house. If it weren't so, would I have told you that I'm going there to prepare a place for you? And once that place is ready, you may be sure that I will come back and take you to be with me. That way we will always be together. You know the way to the place where I am going."

Somewhat confused, Thomas said, "Lord, we aren't sure where you are going, so how can we know the way that will take us there?"

"I am that way," I declared. "I am the truth; I am the life. No one can go to the Father unless he goes through me. If you really knew me, you would know my Father as well. From now on, you do know him, and you have seen him."

Philip said, "Lord, please show us the Father, and then we will be satisfied."

I replied, "Philip, we've been together for a long time. Don't you know by now who I really am? To see me is to see the Father! So how can you say, 'Show us the Father'? Don't you believe that I and the Father are one? I don't speak to you on my own authority. The Father who lives in me is the one who carries out the miraculous deeds you see.

"Believe me when I say that I and the Father are one, or believe it to be true on the basis of the miracles you see me do. I tell you the truth, if you believe in me, you will do the same things that I am doing. In fact, you will do even greater things because I am going away to the Father. And I will do whatever you ask in my name so that the Son may bring glory to the Father. If you ask me for anything in my name, I will do it." *(John 14:1–14)*

THE PROMISE OF THE PARACLETE

"If you love me, you will do what I tell you to do. And I will ask the Father to send you the Holy Spirit to help you and remain with you forever. He is the one who reveals the truth about God. The people of the world reject the Spirit because they neither see him nor know him. But you know him because even now he lives with you and soon will be in your hearts.

"When I go, I will not leave you unprotected, on your own. Besides that, I will come back, just as I promised. In a little while the world won't be able to see me, but you will see me. Because I live, you too will live. Then it will be clear to you that the Father and I are one. Furthermore, you will be one with me and I with you. To know what I have taught and put it into practice is to prove that you love me. If you love me, you will be loved by my Father. I too will love you and reveal myself to you."

The other Judas (not Iscariot) spoke up and asked, "Lord,

I don't understand why you are going to reveal yourself to us but not to others."

I replied, "Those who love me will do what I say. Then my Father will love them, and he and I will come and make our home with them. Those who do not love me will not do what I say. What I am telling you is not something I made up but comes from the Father who sent me.

"I've told you these things while I've been with you. But when I am gone, the Father will send the Holy Spirit to take my place. He will help you remember all that I have said to you and teach you even more." *(John 14:15–26)*

THE GIFT OF PEACE

"The gift I leave with you is peace, the peace that I myself enjoy. It's not the kind of peace the world gives. So don't let your heart be troubled. Don't lose courage.

"Remember what I told you: I am going away, but I will be back. If you really loved me, you would rejoice that I am going to my Father because he is greater than I.

"I have told you this ahead of time, so that when it happens, your faith will not fail. I can't talk with you much longer because the ruler of this world is on his way. But he has no basis for an accusation against me. I am doing exactly what the Father has told me to do. Thus everyone in the world will know that I love the Father.

"It's time to leave; let's be on our way." *(John 14:27–31)*

I AM THE TRUE VINE

"I am the real vine, and my Father is the vine grower. He cuts off every branch that fails to bear fruit, but he prunes every branch that does bear fruit, so it will produce even more. You have been 'pruned' already by the words I have spoken to you.

"It's crucial that you remain in me and I in you. No branch can bear fruit separated from the vine. In the same way you cannot bear fruit unless you remain in me.

"I am the vine and you are the branches. Only if you remain in me and I in you will you be able to bear an abundant crop of fruit. If you break that connection, you can accomplish nothing. If you do not remain in me, you will be thrown aside like a withered branch. Branches like that are picked up and used for firewood.

"If you remain in me and ponder what I have taught you, then whatever you ask for in prayer will be done for you. Would you like to bring honor to my Father? Then bear much fruit and show that you are my disciples." *(John 15:1–8)*

"Abide in My Love"

"My love for you has been the same as the love my Father has for me. Remain true to that love. If you obey my commands you will remain true to my love, just as I obey my Father's commands and remain true to his love. I have told you these things so that you may experience the joy that is mine. I want you to be filled with joy.

"My commandment is that you love one another just as I have loved you. The ultimate proof that a person loves his friend is his willingness to sacrifice his life for him. You will prove your love for me if you do what I command. No longer will I call you servants, because a servant doesn't really know what his master is doing. Rather, I will call you friends because I have shared with you everything my Father has told me.

"It was not you who chose me but I who chose you. I appointed you to go and bear fruit, the kind of fruit that lasts. The Father will give you whatever you ask for in my name. I give you these commands so that you may love one another." *(John 15:9–17)*

THE WORLD WILL HATE YOU

"When you experience the hatred of the world, keep in mind that it hated me before it hated you. If you belonged to the world, the world would love you like one of their own. But you don't belong to the world. I chose you out of the world, and that is why the world hates you. Remember what I told you: 'A servant is not superior to his master.' Since they persecuted me, they will also persecute you. They will respond to your teaching in the same way they responded to mine.

"The people of this world will treat you this way because you belong to me, because they do not know the one who sent me. They would not be guilty of sin if I had not come and spoken to them. As it is, they have no excuse for their sin.

"To hate me is to hate my Father. If I had not performed miraculous deeds that no one else had ever done, they would not be guilty. But they were right there watching and chose to hate both me and my Father. All this happened to fulfill what was written in their law: 'They hated me for no reason.'" *(John 15:18–25)*

THE WITNESS OF THE PARACLETE

"I will send you a Helper, the Spirit of truth who comes from the Father. When he arrives, he will speak on my behalf. You too must speak on my behalf because you have been with me from the beginning of my ministry. *(John 15:26–27)*

ON PERSECUTIONS

"I have told you these things so that nothing will upset your faith. The time will come when you will be expelled from your synagogues. In fact, the time is coming when some of those people will think that by killing you they are doing God a favor. They will do things like that because they have no true knowledge of the Father or of me. I have told you these things so that when the time does come, you will remember what I said would happen." *(John 16:1–4)*

THE WORK OF THE PARACLETE

"Up until now there has been no reason I should have told you these things because I have been with you. But now I am going back to the one who sent me, and not one of you has asked, 'Where are you going?' But because I told you what was going to happen, sorrow has filled your hearts. I tell you the truth: it is to your advantage that I go away. Unless I return to the Father, the Helper will not come to you; but if I go, I will send him to you.

"When the Spirit comes, he will convince the world that they are wrong in their views about sin, righteousness, and judgment. He will convince them that not believing in me is sin. He will convince them that my going to the Father and no longer being in view is proof of my righteousness. He will convince them that judgment is certain because God has already judged the prince of this world.

"I have much more to tell you, but right now it would place too great a burden on you. But when the Spirit comes, he will guide you into a fuller understanding of the truth you have received. He will not speak on his own accord but will pass on to you only what he hears. He will tell you about things yet to come. The Spirit will honor me by taking what I say and explaining it to you. All that the

Father has belongs to me as well. That's why I said that the Spirit will take what I say and explain it to you." *(John 16:5–15)*

SORROW TURNS TO JOY

I continued, "For a short time you won't see me, but after that, you will see me again."

Turning to one another, the disciples asked, "What did he mean when he said, 'For a short time you won't see me, but after that, you will see me again,' and, 'I am going to the Father'?" They kept asking, "What is this 'short time' he keeps talking about? We haven't the faintest idea what he means."

I knew they wanted to question me, so I said, "Are you wondering what I meant when I said, 'For a short time you won't see me, but after that, you will see me again'? I tell you the truth, you will weep and lament like mourners at a funeral, while the world will rejoice. You will be filled with sorrow, but suddenly your sorrow will be transformed into joy.

"When a woman is about to give birth, she is in great pain. But as soon as the child is born, she forgets all about the pain and is filled with joy because she has brought a baby into the world. In the same way for a time you will be in distress. But later I will see you, and your heart will respond with such joy that no one will ever be able to take it from you." *(John 16:16–22)*

PRAY IN MY NAME

"When that day comes, you won't be asking me for anything! I tell you the truth, the Father will grant all that you ask in my name. Until now you haven't asked for anything in this way. So now ask the Father for anything in my name, and you will receive it so that your joy may overflow.

"I have been using figures of speech in talking with you. But the time is coming when what I say will no longer seem obscure. I will be able to explain with clarity about the Father. In the coming age you will ask the Father in my name. I won't have to ask him on your behalf because the Father himself loves you. God loves you because you love me and believe that I came from him. When I came into the world, I left the Father; now I am leaving the world and going back to the Father." *(John 16:23–28)*

THE DISCIPLES TO BE SCATTERED

"Now you are speaking plainly," the disciples said, "and not using figures of speech difficult to understand! Now we know that you know all things, and we do not need to question you any more. For this reason we believe that you truly have come from God."

I replied, "Do you really believe? The time is coming—it's already here—when you will be scattered. Each of you will go to his own home, and I will be left alone. Yet I won't be alone because my Father will be with me. I have told you these things so that, in me, you may have all that makes for true happiness. As long as you are in the world, you will have trouble and sorrow. But cheer up because I have conquered the world!" *(John 16:29–33)*

THE INTERCESSORY PRAYER

When I finished telling the disciples these things, I looked up to heaven and prayed: "Father, the time has now come. Bring glory to your Son so that I can bring glory to you. You have made me sovereign over all mankind so I can give eternal life to everyone you have given to me. Eternal life is learning to know you, the only true God, and me, the one you sent. I've brought glory to you here on earth by completing all you gave me to do. So Father, glorify me now in your presence with the glory I had with you before the world began.

"I have revealed what you are really like to those you took out of the world and gave to me. They were yours, but you gave them to me, and they have obeyed your word. Now they know that you are the source of everything that has come to me. I passed on to them the words you gave me, and they accepted them. They know for sure that I came from you, and they believe that you are the one who sent me. I am not praying for those who belong to this world but for the ones you gave to me. I am praying for them because they belong to you, and glory comes to me through them. Everything I have is yours, and everything you have is mine.

"I am on my way to you, Holy Father. I will no longer remain in this world, but they are still here. Keep them loyal to you (as you have revealed yourself through me) so that they may be one with one another just as you and I are one. When I was with them, I kept them loyal to your revelation through me. Not one of them was lost, except the one destined to be lost, so that what the Scriptures foretold would come true.

"But now I am on my way to you. I have been teaching these things while still in the world so that my followers would experience my joy in all its fullness. I have given them your word, and the world has come to hate them. The reason is obvious: they do not belong to the world any more than I belong to it.

"My prayer is not that you remove them from the world but that you protect them from the evil designs of Satan. They do not belong to this world, just as I do not belong to it. Your word is the truth. Set them apart to yourself by means of the truth. I am sending them into the world just as you sent me. For their sake I consecrate myself to you, that they too may be consecrated by the truth.

"I am not praying for them alone but also for all who will come to believe through what they say about me. I am praying that they may all be one, just as you and I, Father, are one. I pray that they may be one with us so that the people of this world will believe that you sent me.

"I have given them the same glory that you gave to me so that they may be one as we are one—I in them and you in me. I pray that they may be completely one so the people of this world may know that you sent me and that you love them even as you love me.

"Father, I pray that everyone you have given me may be with me wherever I am so that they will see the glory you have given me; for you loved me before the world began. Righteous Father, the world does not know you, but I know you. And those who believe in me know that you have sent me. I made clear to them who you really are, and I will continue to do so. Then the love you have for me will be in them, and I myself will be in them." *(John 17:1–26)*

Chapter Twenty-Six

GETHSEMANE AND MY ARREST

PETER WILL DENY ME

After singing the Passover hymn together, I went, as was my custom, to the Mount of Olives. The disciples followed. While we were on the way, I said to them, "This very night you will all abandon me, for in Scripture God said, 'I will strike the shepherd, and the sheep of the flock will be scattered.' However, after my resurrection I will go to Galilee and meet you there.

"Simon, Simon! Satan has gotten permission to test all of you, to sift you like wheat. But I have prayed for you, Simon, that your faith will not fail, and when you have turned back to me again, you are to strengthen your brothers."

At this, Peter declared, "I will never abandon you, even if the rest of them do! No matter where you go, I will go with you. I will lay down my life for you."

"I tell you the truth, Peter," I responded, "this very night, before the rooster crows, you will have said three times that you do not know me."

But Peter kept protesting, "Lord, I'm ready to go to prison with you, even to die on your behalf!" And all the other disciples said the same. *(Matt. 26:30–35; Mark 14:26–31; Luke 22:31–34, 39; John 13:36–38)*

THE TWO SWORDS

Then I said to them all, "When I sent you out to proclaim the kingdom, you took no coin bag, knapsack, or sandals. Did you lack anything?"

"No, nothing," they replied.

"But in this case, if you have a coin bag, you must take it and likewise a knapsack. If you don't have a sword, sell your coat and buy one. For I tell you that what has been written about me in Scripture—that I would die a shameful death between criminals—must be fulfilled. Indeed, all that was written about me is coming true."

"Look, Lord," said the disciples, "here are two swords!"

"That will do," I said. *(Luke 22:35–38)*

GETHSEMANE

Then we arrived at an olive grove called Gethsemane. I told my disciples, "Sit here while I go a bit further to pray." I took Peter with me, along with James and John, the two sons of Zebedee. Deep distress and anguish rolled over me like a great wave. I let it be known that my soul was crushed with grief, even to the point of death. "Stay here," I told the three disciples, "and keep watch with me. Pray that you won't fail in this crucial time of testing."

Then, leaving the three, I went on a short distance by myself, sank to my knees, and prayed that if possible I might not have to go through the suffering that awaited me. "Dear Father," I prayed, "there is nothing you cannot do. Take this cup of suffering away from me, yet may it be your will that is done, not mine." Just then an angel came from heaven to strengthen me. In great agony I began to pray even more fervently, and my sweat dripped to the ground like heavy drops of blood.

When I arose from prayer, I went back to my disciples and found them asleep, worn out by their grief. To Peter I said, "Simon, how could you go to sleep? Couldn't you watch with me for a single hour? Get up, all of you, and pray that you won't fail in this time of trial. Man's spirit is willing, but human nature is weak." Once again I went off by myself and prayed, "Dear Father, if this cup of suffering cannot be taken away unless I drink it, may your will be done."

When I went back to the disciples a second time, I found them asleep once again, for they were unable to keep their eyes open. They had no excuse for their failure to watch and pray. I returned to my place of prayer and once again yielded myself to the Father's will. I returned for the third time to the disciples and said: "What? Are you still sleeping and taking your rest? Enough of that! The hour has come for the Son of Man to be betrayed into the hands of wicked men. Rouse yourselves! Let's be going. Look, here comes my betrayer." *(Matt. 26:36–46; Mark 14:32–42; Luke 22:39–46; John 18:1)*

MY ARREST

Judas, one of the Twelve, knew about the olive grove, Gethsemane, because I had often met there with my disciples. So he arrived on the scene with a squad of Roman soldiers and temple guards armed with swords and clubs. With them, carrying torches and lanterns, was a rabble crowd that had been incited to action by the leading priests and influential laypeople.

Judas, the one who was about to betray me, had told them, "The man I will greet with a kiss is the one you should arrest and take away under guard." So Judas came straight up to me and said, "Greetings, Rabbi." Then he kissed me.

"My friend," I said, "is it by a kiss that you would betray the Son of Man? Go ahead and do what you came to do."

I knew all that was going to happen so I turned to the mob and said, "Who are you looking for?"

"We are looking for Jesus the Nazarene," they answered.

"I am he," I replied.

At that they all fell back and sank to the ground.

Again I asked, "Who are you looking for?"

"Jesus the Nazarene," they answered.

"I have already told you that I am he. Since I am the one you're looking for, let these men with me go free." I said this so the words of my prayer—"Father, I have not lost a single one of those you gave me"—might come true.

Then the armed crowd grabbed me and put me under arrest. Simon Peter, who was standing close by, drew his sword and took a swing at Malchus, the servant of the high priest, cutting off his right ear.

"Put your sword back where it belongs," I ordered. "Shall I not drink the cup of suffering the Father has given me? All who wield the sword will die by the sword. Don't you understand that if I called on my Father for help, he would without delay send thousands of angels to protect me? But in that case how would the prophetic Scriptures be fulfilled that say this must happen?" Then I touched the servant's ear, and the wound disappeared.

To the leading priests, officers of the temple guard, and

influential laypeople who had taken me into custody, I said, "Why did you come out with swords and clubs to arrest me as though I were some dangerous renegade? Day after day I was right there in the temple courts, teaching, but you didn't lay a hand on me. But this is your moment, the time when darkness reigns. Let the Scripture be fulfilled."

At that my disciples deserted me and ran away. Among them was one young man wearing nothing but a linen loincloth. When they tried to arrest him, he slipped out of their grasp and ran away naked, leaving the linen cloth behind. *(Matt. 26:47–56; Mark 14:43–52; Luke 22:47–53; John 18:2–12)*

BEFORE THE SANHEDRIN

Then they led me off under arrest to Annas, who was the father-in-law of Caiaphas, the high priest that year. Caiaphas had advised the Jewish authorities that it was to their advantage for one man to die for the people.

Peter and John followed the soldiers at a distance as they took me to Annas. Since John was well known by the high priest, they allowed him to enter the courtyard, but Peter had to stay outside near the gate. So John went back out and spoke to the servant girl on duty at the gate. She let Peter come in but asked, "Aren't you also a disciple of that man Jesus?"

"No, I am not," answered Peter.

Since the air was brisk, the servants and temple guards had started a charcoal fire. They were standing around the fire warming themselves, so Peter went over and joined them.

Meanwhile, inside the house, the high priest was questioning me about my disciples and what I had been teaching. I told him, "I have always taught openly where all could hear, in synagogues and in the courts of the temple where people are free to meet. I have said nothing in secret. So, why are you questioning me? The people who have listened to me know what I have been teaching. Why don't you ask them?"

When I said that, one of the guards reached out and slapped me in the face. "How dare you speak to a high priest like that!" he demanded.

I replied, "If I've said something that is not true, produce the evidence. If not, why did you strike me?"

So Annas sent me, still in fetters, to the house of Caiaphas, the high priest, where a number of legal experts and influential laypeople had gathered. Peter was following along some distance behind. When he got to the courtyard of the high priest, he went right in and mingled with the guards. They too had kindled a fire in the center of the courtyard so he sat with them warming himself. He wanted to see how it would all turn out.

The leading priests and the entire Sanhedrin were looking for some kind of evidence against me, whether it was true or not. They needed to construct a case that would warrant the sentence of death. Many gave false witness against me, but their stories didn't agree. Finally two false accusers took the stand and said, "We heard him say, 'I will tear down this temple, made by man, and within three days will build another not made with human hands.'" However, even on this point, their testimonies didn't agree.

Since they were making no progress, the high priest rose before the assembly and asked me, "Are you not going to defend yourself against the charges they're bringing against you?"

I said nothing.

Upset that I wouldn't answer, the high priest put me under oath, saying, "I charge you in the name of the living God—tell us whether you are the Messiah, the Son of God."

I replied, "I am, but not in the way you understand it. The time has come when you will see the Son of Man sitting at the right hand of the Almighty and coming on the clouds of heaven."

"So then, you are the Son of God?" he kept saying.

"It is as you say."

At this the high priest tore his robes and cried out, "Blasphemy! We need no witnesses now. We ourselves have heard it from his own lips! What is your verdict?"

"He's guilty," they all shouted. "He deserves to die." At once the guards began to mistreat me. They spit in my face and beat me with their fists. They blindfolded me and jeered, "Prophesy to us, you Christ! Who hit you that time?" And they kept deriding me with insult after insult. Even the attendants who took me away joined in the abuse. *(Matt. 26:57–68; Mark 14:53–65; Luke 22:54–71; John 18:13–24)*

PETER DENIES ME

Meanwhile Peter was in the courtyard. One of the maids of the high priest caught sight of him in the light of the fire and studied him carefully. Then, going over to where he was sitting, she said, "You were there with Jesus the Galilean!"

Peter denied it before them all, saying, "I haven't the faintest idea of what you're talking about." Then he left the fire and went out into the front courtyard where another maid saw him and said to the men standing around, "This man was with Jesus of Nazareth."

Again Peter denied it, this time with an oath: "I do not know the man!"

About an hour later one of the bystanders, a servant of the high priest and a relative of the man whose ear Peter had cut off, came up and insisted, "We saw you in the olive grove. There's no doubt that you're one of the Galileans, for your accent gives you away."

Then Peter swore, "May God punish me if what I am about to say is not true—I know nothing about this man you're talking about." And while he was speaking, the cock crowed.

Just then I passed through the courtyard and saw Peter. I looked him straight in the eye, and he remembered what I had told him, "Before the cock crows tonight, you will deny me three times." He got up from the fire, went outside, and broke into tears. *(Matt. 26:69–75; Mark 14:66–72; Luke 22:56–62; John 18:25–27)*

DELIVERED TO PILATE

Early in the morning the entire Sanhedrin (leading priests, elders of the people, and legal experts) met to formulate a charge that would force the Roman authorities to put me to death. Then they tied my hands and took me to the headquarters of the Roman military governor. *(Matt. 27:1–2; Mark 15:1; Luke 23:1; John 18:28)*

THE DEATH OF JUDAS

When Judas, the betrayer, learned that I had been condemned, he regretted what he had done. He took the thirty pieces of silver back to the high priests and elders and confessed to them, "What I did was not right. I should not have betrayed an innocent man."

"Why should we care about that?" they answered. "That's your problem, not ours."

So Judas threw the silver coins into the temple, went out, and hanged himself.

The leading priests gathered up the coins and said, "Since this is blood money, it would be against the law to put it into the temple treasury." After discussing the matter, they decided that the money should be used to buy the Potter's field, a place to bury foreigners. That's why, even to this day, it is called the "Field of Blood." This fulfilled the prophecy of Jeremiah, the prophet, who said, "They took the thirty silver coins—the amount the children of Israel had agreed to pay for him—and used them to buy the potter's field, as the Lord had directed me." *(Matt. 27:3–10)*

Chapter Twenty-Seven

THE TRIAL

THE TRIAL BEFORE PILATE

When we arrived at the Roman garrison, the Jewish authorities wouldn't go in because that would be considered ceremonially unclean and would disqualify them for Passover.

So Pilate came out to them and asked, "What charges do you bring against this man?"

"If this man were not a criminal," they said, "we would not be bringing him here to you."

"Take him away and try him according to your own law," said Pilate.

"We can't do that," they admitted, "because we aren't allowed to put anyone to death." (This was to fulfill what I had said about the way I would die.)

Then the religious leaders laid out their case against me, saying, "Here is the man we caught misleading our people, telling them not to pay taxes to Caesar, and claiming that he himself is an anointed king."

So Pilate asked me, "Are you the king of the Jews?"

"The words are yours," I answered. However, when the religious delegation made their accusations against me, I remained silent and would not defend myself.

Pilate asked, "Don't you hear all the charges they're bringing against you?"

To his great surprise, I made no response, not even to a single charge. Turning to my accusers, he said, "I find no reason for punishing this man." Then we went back inside his headquarters where he asked me, "Are you the king of the Jews?"

I answered, "Did you come up with this on your own, or are you parroting what others are saying about me?"

"Do you take me for a Jew?" said Pilate. "It was your own chief priests and people who brought you here to me. You must have done something wrong."

I answered, "My kingdom doesn't belong to this world. If it did, my followers would have fought against the temple guards when they came to arrest me. No, my kingdom is not a political kingdom."

"Ha! So you are a king after all!" exclaimed Pilate.

I answered, "You are the one calling me a king. My purpose for coming into the world has been to declare the truth. Everyone who is on the side of truth pays attention to what I say."

Pilate dismissed the issue with a curt, "And what is truth?" Then he went back outside to the Jewish authorities and reported, "I find no basis at all for a charge against this man."

But the crowds kept pressing their case, claiming, "By his teaching he is causing riots everywhere he goes, from Galilee to Jerusalem." (Matt. 27:11–14; Mark 15:2–5; Luke 23:2–5; John 18:29–38)

HEROD WANTS A MIRACLE

When Pilate heard this, he asked if I were a Galilean, and discovering that I was from a region under the authority of Herod, he sent me to him (Herod was in Jerusalem at that time). Now Herod was delighted with the chance to see me because he had heard about me and for a long time had been anxious to see me perform some miracle. So he asked me question after question, but I would not respond. Meanwhile the religious authorities had gathered around us and were repeating their accusations against me. Before long Herod, and his soldiers as well, began to taunt me. They put a royal robe on me (to ridicule my claim of kingship) and sent me back to Pilate. On that day Herod and Pilate became friends although previously they had been sworn enemies. *(Luke 23:6–12)*

PILATE DECLARES ME INNOCENT

Then Pilate assembled the leading priests, those in positions of authority, as well as the crowd that was involved. He laid out his verdict: "You brought me this man claiming that he was misleading the people. I have examined him openly in your presence and do not find him guilty of any of the charges you bring. Nor did Herod because he released him back to me. This man has done nothing worthy of death so I will have him flogged and then release him." *(Luke 23:13–16)*

JESUS OR BARABBAS?

Each year during Passover it was the custom of the Roman governor to release to the crowd any prisoner they would ask for. At that time they were holding in custody a notorious felon by the name of Barabbas. A large crowd had gathered in front of Pilate's house, so he went out to them and asked, "Which prisoner do you want me to release? Jesus Barabbas or Jesus the king of the Jews? The rebel guilty of murder or the one called Messiah?" (Pilate was fully aware that the Jewish authorities had handed me over for judgment because they were jealous.)

While Pilate was seated on the judgment seat, his wife sent him this message, "Have nothing to do with that innocent man, for I have just suffered a terrible dream about him."

But the religious authorities had stirred up the crowd who kept demanding that Pilate would release Barabbas, not me. "Away with this Galilean," they shouted. "Give us Barabbas." It mattered not to them that the one they called for was in prison for instigating a riot involving murder.

Still hopeful that the crowd would choose Jesus, Pilate asked them one more time: "Which of these two would you like me to set free?"

"Barabbas!" they shouted back.

"In that case," Pilate asked, "what should I do with Jesus who is called Christ, the king of the Jews?"

"Crucify him! Crucify him!" they kept shouting.

Once again Pilate addressed them. "But why should I do that? What crime has he committed? Nothing he has done would merit death. So I will have him flogged and let go."

But they shouted all the more, "Crucify him!" and their relentless clamor won the day. *(Matt. 27:15–23; Mark 16:6–14; Luke 23:17–23; John 18:39–40)*

"BEHOLD THE MAN!"

Then Pilate gave orders to have me severely whipped. Some troops from the Roman legion took me into the courtyard of the

Praetorium, the official residence of the governor. They invited the rest of the detachment to join them in making sport of me. They stripped off my clothes and draped a cheap scarlet robe around my shoulders. Then they twisted some thorny branches into a crown and pressed it down on my head. They put a staff in my right hand and, falling at my feet, mocked me, saying, "Long live the King of Jews!" They spit on me. They took the staff and beat me over the head. Having grown weary of the charade, they removed the scarlet robe and put my own clothes back on me.

Once again Pilate went out before the crowd. "Listen!" he said, "I will have Jesus brought out to you, but I want you to know that I find no basis for a charge against him."

I came out, wearing the crown of thorns and the purple robe. "Look! Here is the man!" declared Pilate.

When the chief priests and their temple guards saw me, they shrieked, "Crucify him! Crucify him!!"

"No," said Pilate, "you take him and crucify him! I find no basis for a charge against him."

The Jewish authorities answered back, "We have a law that is punishable by death, and he broke it. He claimed to be the Son of God."

This gave Pilate yet another reason to be afraid. So he went back inside and asked me, "Where are you from, really?"

I gave him no answer.

"Why won't you answer my question?" said Pilate. "Don't you know that I have the authority to set you free or to crucify you?"

"If God had not given you the authority," I answered, "you wouldn't be able to do anything to me. So the one who handed me over to you is guilty of an even greater sin."

Pilate continued to try to set me free. But the Jewish authorities kept shouting, "If you let this man go, you are no friend of the emperor! Anyone who claims to be king is guilty of rebellion against the emperor!"

When Pilate heard this implied threat, he brought me out and took his seat on the judges' bench. The place was called "The Stone Pavement" or, in the language of the Jews, "Gabbatha." It was about noon on the day before Passover (the day of preparation). "Here is your king!" said Pilate to the mob.

"Away with him! Away with him!" they shouted. "Crucify him!"

"So you want me to crucify him?" responded Pilate in mock astonishment.

"The only king we have is the emperor!" shouted back the chief priests. *(Matt. 27:27–31a; Mark 15:16–20a; John 19:1–15)*

PILATE DELIVERS ME TO BE CRUCIFIED

When Pilate realized that he was getting nowhere—in fact, a riot was breaking out—he took some water, washed his hands in full view of the people, and declared, "I have no responsibility for what you intend to do to this man. His blood is on your hands; mine are clean."

And the whole crowd yelled back, "Let his blood be on us and on our children!"

So Pilate, not wanting any further commotion, released to them Barabbas, the man who had been put into prison for insurrection and murder. Then he had me flogged and turned over to the soldiers to do whatever the religious authorities wished. *(Matt. 27:24–26; Mark 15:15; Luke 23:24–25; John 19:16)*

Chapter Twenty-Eight

THE CRUCIFIXION

THE ROAD TO GOLGATHA

Then they led me out of the courtyard to the place where they would crucify me. As we were on our way to Golgotha, the guards laid hold of a man named Simon who was coming in from the countryside. He was the father of Alexander and Rufus and came from Cyrene in North Africa. They made him carry my cross and follow along behind. A huge crowd of people followed us, including some women who were beating their breasts and mourning for me. I turned to them and said, "Daughters of Jerusalem, don't weep for me; weep rather for yourselves and for your children. The days are coming when people will say, 'How fortunate are women who have never given birth, wombs that have never born children, breasts that have never nursed!' People will come to the point of saying to the mountains, 'Fall on us!' and to the hills, 'Cover us up!' If God does this when the tree is green, what will he do when it turns dry? That is, if he allows his anointed one to suffer like this, how much more will an impenitent nation suffer in the coming judgment."

Two others, who were criminals, were led away with me to be put to death. *(Matt. 27:31b–32; Mark 15:20b–21; Luke 23:26–32; John 19:17a)*

THE CRUCIFIXION

When we arrived at the place of execution, "The Skull" (or Golgatha, as it is known in the Jewish language), the soldiers offered me some wine mixed with a drug called myrrh. I took a sip, but it was too bitter to drink. Then they nailed me to the cross between two criminals, one on my right, the other on my left.

"Father, forgive them," I prayed, "they don't know what they are doing." It was about nine in the morning.

Above my head Pilate nailed a board that read, "Jesus of Nazareth, the King of the Jews." It was written in Aramaic, Latin, and Greek so all could understand. Many of the people in Jerusalem read this inscription because the place where I was crucified was just outside the city. The chief priests went to Pilate and said, "Why did you write, 'The King of the Jews'? You should have written, 'This man claimed to be the King of the Jews.'"

Pilate answered, "What I have written stays written."

After the soldiers had nailed me to the cross, they took my robe and tore it into four pieces, one piece for each of them. Since my inner garment was seamless, woven from top to bottom, the soldiers said to one another, "Let's not rip it apart but throw dice to see who will get it." This happened so the Scripture would be fulfilled that said, "They divided up my robe, but threw dice for my inner garment."

When I saw my mother standing there with John by her side, I said to her, "Mother dear, John is now your son!" Then I said to John, "My mother Mary is now your mother!" On that very day

John took her home to live as part of his family. *(Matt. 27:33–37; Mark 15:22–26; Luke 23:33–34; John 19:17b–27)*

DERIDED ON THE CROSS

As people passed by the cross, they reviled me, shaking their heads in mockery and hurling insults, "You who would destroy the temple and rebuild it in three days," they taunted, "save yourself. If you're the Son of God, come on down from the cross."

The leading priests, along with the legal experts and influential members of the Sanhedrin joined with the crowd. "He saved others," they scoffed, "but he can't save himself! Isn't he supposed to be the King of Israel?" they asked in mock surprise. "If he comes down from the cross, we will believe in him. He has put his faith in God; let God deliver him now . . . if he wants to. For he said, 'I am God's son!'" *(Matt. 27:38–43; Mark 15:27–32a; Luke 23:35–38)*

THE TWO THIEVES

The soldiers also mocked me, coming up and jeering, "If you are the King of the Jews, save yourself!"

One of the two criminals hanging there kept reviling me, "Aren't you the Messiah? Then prove it by saving yourself and us too!"

The other criminal rebuked him saying, "Don't you have any fear of God, even when you are about to die? We deserve death for the crimes we've committed, but this man has done nothing wrong." Then, turning to me, he asked, "Please remember me when you come as King."

And I assured him, "This very day you will be with me in paradise." *(Matt. 27:44; Mark 15:32b; Luke 23:33–43)*

MY DEATH

About noon the sun's light began to fail, and a deep darkness settled over the entire land until three in the afternoon. At that time I cried out with a loud voice in Aramaic, *"Eli, Eli, lema sabach-thani?"* That is, "My God, my God, why have you forsaken me?"

Some of those standing nearby heard my cry, and said, "Listen, this man is calling for Elijah."

Knowing that my work on earth was complete, I said, "I am thirsty."

One of the men standing there ran and soaked a sponge with sour wine, and using the branch of a hyssop plant, held it up to my mouth so I could moisten my lips.

"Wait," said the others, "Let's see if Elijah will come and take him off the cross."

Once again I raised my voice and cried out, "Father, into your hands I yield my spirit." As I took my last breath, the veil in the sanctuary was suddenly ripped from top to bottom. At the same time the earth shook violently, massive rock formations were shattered, graves broke open, and many of God's people who had died were raised to life. (After I was raised, these saints came out of the tombs and went into Jerusalem, the Holy City, where they appeared to many people.)

When the Roman captain, and the other troops assigned to guard me, saw the earthquake and everything that had happened, they were frightened and exclaimed, "Beyond all doubt this man was God's Son! He is not guilty of the charges leveled against him." When the crowd that had gathered to watch me be put to death saw what had taken place, they returned to the city beating their breasts in sorrow. *(Matt. 27:45–54; Mark 15:33–39; Luke 23:44–48; John 19:28–30)*

WITNESSES OF MY CRUCIFIXION

But my friends, including the women who had followed me from Galilee ministering to my needs, remained at a distance and continued to watch. Among them were my mother Mary and her sister Salome (the wife of Zebedee and mother of James and John), Mary the wife of Clopas (and mother of James the younger and Joseph), and Mary Magdalene. *(Matt. 27:55–56; Mark 15:40–41; Luke 23:49; John 19:25–27)*

MY SIDE IS PIERCED

Since it was Friday, the Jewish authorities asked Pilate to have the legs of the crucified men broken and their bodies taken down. They didn't want us on the cross during the Sabbath, especially during Passover. So the soldiers came and broke the legs of the two men who had been crucified with me. But when they came to me, they could see that I had already died. So they didn't break my legs.

But one of the soldiers did thrust a spear into my side, and at once blood and water flowed out. The disciples knew this to be true because it was reported by a reliable witness who actually saw it happen. So now all of them may believe it. This happened so that the Scripture would be fulfilled, "Not one of his bones will be broken," and, "They will look on him in whose side they thrust a spear." *(John 19:31–37)*

MY BURIAL

Joseph of Arimathea was a highly respected member of the Jewish court, a good and upright man, and also one of my followers. He did not openly acknowledge this relationship because he feared what the religious authorities might do. However, in this case, he decided to go to Pilate and ask for my body.

Since it was Friday, the day of preparation, and tomorrow would be the Sabbath when no work could be done, it was essential that my body be taken down by sunset. Joseph was looking forward to the coming kingdom of God and therefore had not consented to the plans the religious leaders had made against me. So he went to Pilate and asked for my body, a request that took considerable courage.

Pilate had his doubts whether I could have died so soon, so he sent for the Roman officer in charge to ask if I were already dead. When the officer reported that I had died, Pilate gave Joseph permission to take my body. So Joseph took it down from the cross. Nicodemus [the Pharisee who sometime before had visited me at night] had come bringing about seventy-five pounds of spices, a mixture of myrrh and aloes. The two men wrapped my body in a linen shroud, interlayered with spices, as required by the Jewish burial customs. Near the place where I was crucified was a garden in which Joseph had his own rock-hewn tomb that had never been used. Since the Sabbath was about to begin, they placed my body in the tomb, rolled a large disklike stone across the opening, and left.

Mary Magdalene and Mary the mother of Jesus, having followed along, took note of the tomb where my body was placed. Then they returned home and prepared spices and ointments for burial. Since the Sabbath had come, they took their rest as Jewish law required. *(Matt. 27:57–61; Mark 15:42–47; Luke 23:50–56; John 19:38–42)*

The Guard at the Tomb

On the following day, the Sabbath, the leading priests and Pharisees went in a group to Pilate. "Your Excellency," they said, "we recall that while that impostor was still alive he said that after three days he would rise from the dead. So we are asking you to have the tomb securely guarded until that time has passed. Otherwise, his disciples may come and steal his body and then claim that he has risen from the dead. Such a deception would be worse than the previous one."

"You have a guard of soldiers," Pilate told them. "Go and make it as secure as you know how." Then they went and made the tomb secure by sealing the stone and setting the guard. *(Matt. 27:62–66)*

Chapter Twenty-Nine

THE RESURRECTION AND APPEARANCES

THE EMPTY TOMB

Saturday evening, when the Sabbath was over, Mary Magdalene, Mary the mother of James, and Salome went out and bought some aromatic oils, intending to come and anoint my body. Early the following morning the two Marys arrived at the tomb, and to their surprise there had been a great earthquake. An angel of the Lord had come down from heaven, rolled the stone away, and was sitting on it. His face shown like a flash of lightning, and his robe was as white as snow. The guards were paralyzed with fear and had fallen to the ground like dead men.

On the way to the tomb, the women had been asking one another, "Who will roll the stone away from the entrance to the tomb? It is far too heavy for us." But upon arriving, they saw that the stone had already been rolled to one side. So they entered the tomb only to discover that my body was no longer there. While they were standing there perplexed, suddenly there appeared angelic beings in dazzling attire. Full of fear, the women bowed with their faces to the ground. The angels said, "There is no reason to be afraid; I know you are looking for Jesus of Nazareth who was crucified. But the living are not found among the dead. Jesus is not here; he is risen! Look, there is the niche where they placed him. Now we want you to go quickly and tell Peter and the others that Jesus has risen from the dead. He will go to Galilee and be there to meet you, just as he promised. Remember how, before he left Galilee, he told you that the Son of man must be betrayed into the hands of sinful men, be crucified, and three days later be raised from the dead."

Leaving the tomb, trembling with excitement, the women ran quickly to tell the eleven disciples, but Mary remained outside the tomb weeping. Still in tears, she bent down to look inside. There she saw two angels dressed in white sitting where my body had been, one at my head and the other at my feet. "Woman, why are you weeping?" they asked her.

Mary answered, "They have taken away my Master, and I don't know where they've put him." She glanced over her shoulder and saw me standing there but didn't recognize me.

I asked, "Woman, why are you weeping? Who are you looking for?"

Thinking that I was the gardener, she said, "Sir, if you are the one who took him away, tell me where you put him, so I can go and get him."

Then I said to her, "Mary!"

She turned to me and cried out in Aramaic, *"Rabbouni!"* [the word means "Teacher"].

"You don't need to hold on to me!" I said, "for I haven't yet ascended to my Father. But go to my disciples and tell them, 'I am returning to my Father and God, and to your Father and God.'"

While the women were on their way to tell the disciples what had happened, suddenly I was there in their path. "May you be filled with joy!" I exclaimed. They ran to me, fell to the ground, clasping my feet, and worshipped me.

"Don't be afraid," I said to them; "Go and tell my disciples to set out for Galilee; they will see me there."

When the women arrived with good news, Mary Magdalene was the first to exclaim, "I have seen the Master!" Then she and the other women (Joanna, Mary the mother of James, and several more) told the disciples everything that had happened. To the apostles their report seemed like an idle tale and difficult to believe.

However, Peter and John left to find out for themselves. They left together, but John (the younger) outran Peter and got there first. Bending down to peer inside, he could see the linen cloths in place but didn't go in.

But when Simon Peter came running up, he went straight into the tomb. He, too, saw the linen grave-clothes and the burial cloth that had been wound around my head. (It was not with the other wrappings but folded up and lying by itself.) Then John, who had arrived first at the tomb, went inside. When he saw that the tomb was empty, he believed Mary's report. (As yet the disciples did not understand from Scripture that I would rise from the dead.) *(Matt. 28:1–10; Mark 16:1–8; Luke 24:1–12; John 20:1–18)*

GUARDS TO CLAIM MY BODY STOLEN

While the women were still on their way, some of the soldiers assigned to guard the tomb went into Jerusalem and told the leading priests everything that had happened. The priests met with the elders and devised a plan. The guards were to claim that during the night, while they were sleeping, my disciples came and stole my body. For this they would receive a considerable amount of money. If the governor happened to hear about this, the priests and elders would convince him that the guards were blameless. So there was no reason to be concerned. The soldiers accepted the bribe and did what they were told. This story has circulated among the Jews ever since. *(Matt. 28:11–15)*

I APPEAR TO TWO DISCIPLES ON THEIR WAY TO EMMAUS

On that same day two of my followers were on their way to Emmaus, a village some seven miles from Jerusalem. As they walked along, discussing everything that had recently happened in the city, I joined them on their journey. They did not recognize me, for God had touched their eyes. I inquired of them, "What have you two been discussing so seriously as you walk along?"

They stopped in their tracks, faces filled with grief. One of them, Cleopas by name, said, "You must be the only person visiting Jerusalem who is unaware of what has been going on there these past few days."

"What would that be?" I asked.

"Haven't you heard what happened to the man from Nazareth called Jesus?" they asked. "He proved himself a prophet by his powerful acts and teaching before God and all the people. Our religious leaders turned him over to the Roman authorities to be sentenced to death and crucified. We had hoped he would be the one sent by God to set our nation free, but he was put to death, and that was three days ago. But that's not all! Early this morning some women in our group went to his tomb but couldn't find his body. Returning, they told of a vision in which angels said he was alive. So some others in the group went straight to the tomb; and, as the women had reported, his body was nowhere to be found."

At that point I said to them, "You foolish men! You find it so difficult to believe all that the prophets wrote in Scripture. Was it not necessary for the Messiah to suffer as he did before entering his glorious reign?" Then I explained to them every passage of Scripture—from the books of Moses and all the prophets—that spoke of me.

As we approached the village where they were going, I acted as if I intended to continue on. But they urged me to stay with them, saying, "The day is almost over, and it is getting dark."

So I went to where the two men lived. At dinner that evening, I took the bread and blessed it. Breaking it in pieces, I handed it to them. Then their eyes were opened, and they realized who I was. But at that moment I disappeared from their sight.

Cleopas and his companion said to each other, "Did not our hearts burn within us as he spoke to us along the road, explaining Scripture?" So they rose from the table without delay and set out for Jerusalem. Upon arriving, they went to where the Eleven had gathered with friends. The disciples exclaimed to the visitors, "The Lord is risen! No doubt about it! He has appeared to Peter!"

Then Cleopas and his companion told the gathering what had happened on the road and how they had come to recognize me when I was at their house for dinner and began to break the bread. *(Luke 24:13–35)*

I Appear to Disciples, Thomas Absent

The disciples were together in Jerusalem behind locked doors for fear of the Jewish authorities. Suddenly I was standing there in their midst.

"Peace be with you!" I said. They were terrified, thinking that I was a ghost.

I asked, "Why are you so alarmed, and why do you wonder who I am? Look at my hands and my feet; it is actually I! Touch me and you will find out; no ghost has flesh and bones like this." Then I showed them my hands and my feet. They still couldn't accept the fact that it was I, so full of joy and amazement were they.

So I asked them, "Do you have anything here to eat?"

They handed me a piece of broiled fish, which I took and ate right before their eyes.

I said, "This is what I meant when I was still with you and said, 'Everything written about me in the law of Moses, the prophets, and the Psalms must come to pass.'" Then I opened their minds so they could understand the Scriptures. I said, "Thus it is written, 'The Messiah must suffer and die and on the third day rise again.' It is also written that the message of repentance and the forgiveness of sins be proclaimed in my name to all nations, beginning in Jerusalem. You are to be witnesses of all these things, and I will provide you with the promised Holy Spirit. For now, however, wait here in Jerusalem until the Spirit comes from heaven to fill you with power."

"Peace be with you!" I said again and added, "I am now sending you, just as the Father sent me." Then I breathed on them and said, "Receive the Holy Spirit. If you forgive anyone's sins, they are forgiven; but if you do not forgive their sins, they are not forgiven." *(Luke 24:36–53; John 20:19–23)*

I APPEAR TO DISCIPLES, THOMAS PRESENT

Although Thomas (called "The Twin") was one of the Twelve, he was not with them when I suddenly appeared. They kept telling him, "We have seen the Lord!"

His response was: "Unless I see the wounds where the nails were driven through his hands and touch them with my own finger,

I will never believe it. I will have to put my hand into his side where the spear drew blood."

A week later they were together in the house, and this time Thomas was there. Again I appeared in their midst, although the doors were closed and securely locked.

"Peace be with you!" I said. Then turning to Thomas, I said, "Put your finger here where the nails were driven through. Put your hand into my side. Stop doubting and learn to trust."

Thomas exclaimed, "It is you! My Lord and my God!"

I said, "Thomas, you believe because you have seen me. Blessed are those who will come to believe without ever having seen me." *(John 20:24–29)*

I APPEAR TO THE DISCIPLES BY THE SEA OF TIBERIUS

Later on I appeared to the disciples on the shore of Lake Tiberius. This is what happened. Simon Peter, Thomas (the Twin), Nathanael (from Cana in Galilee), John and his brother James (sons of Zebedee), and two other disciples were there. Peter announced, "I'm going out to fish."

"We'll go with you," said the others. So they got into a boat and went out to fish but didn't catch a thing all night long.

Early the following morning I was standing on the shore, but they didn't recognize me. So I called out to them, "Hey there! Did you catch anything?"

"No," they shouted back.

So I told them, "Cast your net to the right side, and you'll get a catch."

They did what I said and caught so many fish they were unable to hoist the net into the boat.

Suddenly John realized that I was the person standing on the shore. He said to Peter, "It's the Lord!" When Simon Peter heard this, he wrapped his outer garment around him (he had stripped for work), and plunged into the lake. Since they were not far from land (about a hundred yards), the rest of them followed in the boat, dragging the net full of fish.

When they landed, they saw a charcoal fire with fish cooking on it. There was some bread as well.

"Bring me some of the fish you've just caught," I told them.

So Simon Peter climbed back into the boat and dragged the net onto the sand. It was full of large fish, 153, to be exact. Even though the catch was so large, the net had not ripped apart.

I said to them, "Come, let's have breakfast." Not one of them ventured to ask, "Who are you?" because they were all sure that it was I. Picking up the bread, I walked over and handed it to them. I did the same with the fish. This was one of the times I appeared to them after I was raised from the dead.

When we had finished eating, I said to Simon Peter, "Simon, son of John, do you love me more than these?"

"Yes, Lord," replied Peter, "you know that I love you."

"Then feed my lambs."

I asked a second time, "Simon, son of John, do you love me?"

"Yes, Lord," replied Peter, "you know that I love you."

"Then be a shepherd to my sheep," I said.

Yet a third time I asked, "Simon, son of John, do you love me?"

Peter was distressed that I had asked him three times if I loved him. "Lord," he said, "you know everything; you know that I love you."

I replied, "Then feed my sheep. I tell you the truth, when you were a young man, you used to dress yourself and go wherever you wanted. But when you are old, you will stretch out your hands so someone else can dress you and carry you where you'd rather not go." [I said this to indicate the kind of death Peter would die to bring honor to God.] Then I said to Peter, "Follow me!"

As we walked along, Peter glanced back and saw that John was following us. (John was the one who leaned back against me during our last supper and asked, "Lord, who is it that will betray you?") So Peter asked, "Lord, what will happen to John?"

I replied, "Even if he should remain alive until I return, what difference would that make for you?" So the rumor spread among the early believers that John would not die. But I did not say that he would not die. I simply said, "Even if he should remain alive until I return, what difference would that make for you?" *(John 21:1–19)*

THE GREAT COMMISSION

Following this, the eleven disciples went to Galilee, to the mountain where I had arranged to meet them. When they saw me, they bowed in worship, although some wondered whether it was really I. Stepping forward, I said, "All authority in heaven and on earth has been given to me; therefore go and make disciples in every nation. Baptize them in the name of the Father, the Son, and the Holy Spirit, and teach them to obey all the commands I have given you. And remember, I will be with you always, even to the close of the age." *(Matt. 28:16–20)*

THE ASCENSION

At a later date I left Jerusalem with my disciples and went as far as Bethany. Lifting my hands to heaven, I gave them my blessing. During this act of blessing, I was raised from their midst and carried up into heaven. They bowed down in worship and then returned with great joy to Jerusalem. Day after day they were in the temple courts blessing God. *(Luke 24:50–53)*

CONCLUDING STATEMENT

The disciples watched me perform many other miracles that are not included in this account, but if they were all written down, I don't think the world itself would be big enough to hold all the books. But the miracles you have read are included so you will come to believe that I am the Messiah, the Son of God. By believing that I am who I say I am, you will receive eternal life. *(John 21:24–25; 20:30–31)*

INDEX

Do you believe in wind?

Can you see the wind?
You can see what it does.
Sometimes you need a strong
wind to move things.
Sometimes a gentle breeze of wind
can bring a cool relief on a hot day.

You can't always see God,
but you see Him move things!
He is like the wind!!